# A Shepherd's Care

## Reflections on the Changing Role of Pastor

Bishops' Committee
on Priestly Life and Ministry
National Conference
of Catholic Bishops

In its 1985 planning document, as approved by the general membership of the National Conference of Catholic Bishops in November 1984, the Bishop's Committee on Priestly Life and Ministry, through its Secretariat, was authorized to address the office of the pastor and his changing role in the Church in the United States. A draft was reviewed by the Administrative Committee in March 1987. The following text has been approved by Bishop Thomas J. Murphy, Chairman of the Priestly Life and Ministry Committee, and authorized for publication by the undersigned.

Monsignor Daniel F. Hoye
General Secretary
May 19, 1987                                          NCCB/USCC

ISBN 1-55586-166-0

# Contents

# Acknowledgments

The Bishops' Committee on Priestly Life and Ministry of the National Conference of Catholic Bishops presents *A Shepherd's Care: Reflections on the Changing Role of Pastor.*

In so doing, it wishes to express deep appreciation to the members of the ad hoc writing committee that developed the document in its present form: Bishop W. Thomas Larkin, St Petersburg, chairman; Bishop Emerson J. Moore, New York; Reverends Curtis Halfmann, Lubbock; Brian T. Joyce, Oakland; John F. Kinsella, Baltimore; Reid C. Mayo, Burlington; Frank J. McNulty, Newark; Dennis M. Metzger, Toledo; Robert F. Pfeiffer, Cleveland; and Rev. Msgr. Colin A. MacDonald, executive director of the Committee Secretariat.

The Committee is especially grateful for the contribution of Fr. Kinsella who served as principal writer during the various stages of the document's development. It also wishes to acknowledge the work of Msgr. MacDonald who was charged with its preparation for publication.

The formation of this document began in 1984 when the Committee was chaired by Bishop Michael J. Murphy, Erie. We are grateful to him for his vision and leadership in giving initial impetus to this project.

The writing committee first developed a questionnaire on the role of the pastor. This was circulated to priests, religious, deacons, and laity of selected archdioceses, dioceses, and religious communities. The results of this survey were very important in the development of the initial draft.

A most valuable contribution to the formation of the document was provided by the National Federation of Priests Councils. Its

1985 national convention: "The Pastor in an Age of Challenge" provided much useful information. At that time, the NFPC also circulated the questionnaire to the delegates in attendance and compiled the responses for committee use. The Bishops' Committee on Priestly Life and Ministry extends a special thanks to the NFPC for its gracious assistance in this matter.

Of particular mention are the priests of the Archdiocese of Chicago. Under the direction of Rev. Thomas F. Ventura, over one hundred of them responded to the questionnaire, providing added material for the writing committee.

During the course of the written consultation, the committee engaged in interviews with experts in various fields: Mrs. Dolores Leckey, Laity; Sr. Jo Ann Miller, OSF, Human Resources for Ministry; Reverends Gerard T. Broccolo, Liturgy; John J. Myers, Canon Law; Philip J. Murnion, National Pastoral Life Center; and Thomas J. Sweetser, SJ, Parish Evaluation Project. Their cooperation and assistance are deeply appreciated.

The Committee also wishes to thank two organizations that have provided important assistance and support to this project: Foundations and Donors Interested in Catholic Activities, Inc. (FADICA) and the National Organization for the Continuing Education of Roman Catholic Clergy (NOCERCC). FADICA provided sponsorship for a symposium on the pastor; NOCERCC developed programs for the implementation of A Shepherd's Care.

This document is the culmination of over three years work by the writing committee. In the course of its five drafts, the paper has been brought to the attention of many individuals, and we are grateful to all who assisted in its formation.

Prior to its final form, it was critiqued by the NCCB/USCC Advisory Council and the Administrative Committee of Bishops. It is now presented to the Church in the United States as an "unfinished" document. It is the hope of the Bishops' Committee on Priestly Life and Ministry that pastors themselves, in dialogue with their people and through quality pastoring, will provide the ongoing conclusion envisioned by A Shepherd's Care: Reflections on the Changing Role of Pastor.

## Bishops' Committee on Priestly Life and Ministry (1985-1988)

Most Rev. Thomas J. Murphy
Chairman
Most Rev. John R. Quinn
Most Rev. W. Thomas Larkin
Most Rev. William S. Skylstad
Most Rev. John J. McRaith
Most Rev. Thomas J. Costello
Most Rev. John H. Ricard
Most Rev. Leo E. O'Neil
Most Rev. Robert F. Morneau

Msgr. Colin A. MacDonald
Executive Director
Rev. Richard P. Hynes
Rev. Michael A. Jamail
Rev. Henry Greiner
Rev. Dennis M. Metzger
Rev. Thomas J. Singer, OMI
Rev. Robert J. Cook
Rev. John R. Gilbert
Rev. P. Michael Galvan
Rev. James M. Petonic
Rev. Thomas G. Ogg

### Subcommitee Members

Rev. J. Cletus Kiley
Rev. David E. Brinkmoeller

# I. Introduction

> For we have every confidence that the Church in the light of this
> Council will gain in spiritual riches. New sources of energy will be
> open to her, enabling her to face the future without fear.[1]

Pope John XXIII opened the Second Vatican Council with these
optimistic words, and he and the bishops of the world began an
ambitious program of renewal that was to affect every aspect of
church life. While all of the people of God were given the charge
to develop "new sources of energy" from the deliberations of the
council fathers, the grass-roots implementation of council policy
and the particular task of introducing changes in worship, religious
education, and parish government in the local Church fell largely
to the pastor. Because of this responsibility, pastors have become
figures of great controversy—sometimes deeply loved, sometimes
greatly criticized, but seldom ignored.

If one looks through the literature on the post-Vatican II Church,
there is a wealth of material about parish life, religious education,
sacramental ministry, and even about priesthood itself; but the role
and function of the pastor are usually given marginal treatment.
There are few works written exclusively about the role of the pastor,
and there is even less about the lived experience of pastoring over
the past two decades. What has happened is still mainly an oral
tradition.

---

1. Pope John XXIII, "Opening Address to the Second Vatican Council,"
October 11, 1962.

1

It was this gap, this lack of a systematic analysis of the experience of post-Vatican II pastors, that prompted the Committee on Priestly Life and Ministry to undertake this project. What underlies this effort is the conviction that, while there are some sad failures, there are ever so many heroic stories to be told. The combination of heroism and generosity, contrasted with personal suffering, makes the experience of the changing nature and shape of the pastorate after the Vatican Council worth describing in detail.

## Method, Audience, and Purpose

This paper will chronicle the experience of pastors in the United States over the past twenty years by offering an extended reflection on the changing nature of their ministry—how their roles, their relationships, and their environment have been transformed. The reflection will extend into the future by identifying elements now in place that will shape the pastorate of tomorrow.

The Committee on Priestly Life and Ministry has in the past conducted sociological research and analysis on priestly issues,[2] but it has chosen in this instance rather to listen informally to the voices of pastors themselves. These extended reflections are based on their insights and on a more concentrated and structured dialogue with pastors, bishops, and those who have worked closely with pastors.

One important reason for choosing the method of extended reflection—a slightly disciplined way of thinking out loud—has to do with the nature of the evolutionary process the pastorate has experienced since Vatican II. As those who lived through it know well, the implementation of Vatican II was not systematic. No one sat down with the documents of Vatican II, read out the implications for pastor and pastoral leadership, redefined his role, and retrained him for his part in renewal. The experience was much more dynamic and, at times, chaotic and, of necessity, experimental.

---

2. For two examples of such research-based studies, see NCCB Committee on Priestly Life and Ministy, *Fullness in Christ: A Report on a Study of Clergy Retirement,* 1978; and NCCB Committee on Priestly Life and Ministry, *The Health of American Catholic Priests,* 1985 (Washington, D.C.: USCC Office of Publishing and Promotion Services).

2

Young pastors, especially those ordained well after the Second Vatican Council concluded in 1966, were not part of many of the earlier experiences described here. This retrospective method, however, does serve to underscore the very essential point that the pastorate, as we know it, is the fruit of hard-won experience and experimentation.

If this paper is not a technical, sociological essay, it is even less a theological and scriptural study. What will be described in these pages makes sense only in the context of faith. Pastors, like all priests, are meant to draw strength from their faith. Most are conscious that they have been called to a special way of life, to a unique identity with Christ the High Priest that enables them to serve their people in a special way. They are meant to love and cherish their sharing in the ministerial priesthood and to see it as a great gift from God not only for themselves but for the Church. They draw vision from the Gospel and teachings of the Church, and they attempt to share that vision with their people. They draw their sense of purpose from the mission of Christ and their call to promote that mission. However, a systematic and thoughtful review of this faith and gospel dimension of the pastorate will not be presented here; in a sense, it will be assumed.

The primary audience that the Committee on Priestly Life and Ministry hopes to reach with these reflections is pastors themselves and those who will be pastors some day. The former have been the authors and creators of the renewed role of pastor; the latter will build on the foundations their predecessors have fashioned. It is the conviction of this Committee that pastors seldom indulge in the wholesome and legitimate exercise of positive reflection on their significant accomplishments of the past twenty years. They are, more often than not, conscious of the failed experiments and the sharp criticisms they receive from many sources. Pastors frequently describe themselves as feeling overwhelmed by particularly difficult problems or by a general sense of the magnitude of their responsibilities. A thoughtful, sustained review of the transformed and transforming ministry of the pastorate may add perspective to those who feel discouraged. It may give them a well-deserved sense of accomplishment.

It is for these reasons that this paper has concentrated on the pastor. This is not to denigrate the role of associates or parochial vicars, for there is much in this paper that can be helpful to them. Rather, the Committee chose to reflect here on the office of pastor, especially his contribution to renewal since Vatican II and the

3

importance of his position within the Church of the present and for the future.

Consequently, it is the hope of the Committee on Priestly Life and Ministry that these reflections will capture the experience of the renewal of the pastorate. It is hoped, too, that this effort will affirm and encourage those many pastors who, through their dedication, have accomplished this renewal.

# II. Transformations: The Pastorate 1967-1987

It has been observed that the Second Vatican Council recast the role of the bishop and the role of the laity in very fundamental ways. For the bishops, the notion of collegiality served as a basis for redefining their relationship to the pope and to each other. For the laity, the theology of the "people of God" and their rightful role within the Church elevated their self-perception and transformed their relationship to the whole community of the Church.

The Council did not, however, reconceptualize the role of priest or pastor. In regard to the priest, it repeated and summed up the best of the tradition of the Catholic Church. The Council said very little explicitly about the role of pastor. The document on the priesthood *Decree on the Ministry and Life of Priests,* unlike some other documents of Vatican II, was not followed by an implementing document.

For pastors, the renewal of Vatican II lacked a coherent conceptual framework for a renewed self-definition. They were given the task of initiating and implementing this renewal. Their redefinition, therefore, arose as much out of the experience of implementation as out of the theology of the conciliar documents. As they became agents of change, most pastors changed their own function and identity as well.

The transformation of the pastorate after Vatican II was, as has been observed, not an orderly event. But, it can be described as a series of changes—changes in role, in relationships, in environment, and in personal and spiritual dimensions.

## A. Changing Roles

The fundamental role and functions of the pastor—leadership, teaching, and pastoral care[3]—were the same in 1967 and 1987. Indeed, they have their roots in the mandate of Christ to his disciples and in the earliest understanding of the Christian community of itself. What has changed, however, is the manner in which these functions are carried out as well as the needs of the people of the Catholic community.

### 1. Leadership

From the earliest days of the Church, the presiding elder of the Christian community was called upon to be a leader of the people (see 1 Tm 3:1-7). The pastor of the contemporary American parish has seen his leadership role shaped and formed in recent years by a series of factors: the demands of liturgical renewal; the participative mood of his increasingly well-educated people; the spiritual hunger in a secularized society; and changing parish and neighborhood conditions. These factors have led pastors to emphasize and reformulate three areas of leadership: spiritual leadership, community leadership, and administrative leadership.

#### a. Spiritual Leadership

Prior to Vatican II, the spiritual role of the pastor focused on his administration of the sacraments and his promotion of devotions that sustained spiritual growth. The renewal of Vatican II has expanded the role of spiritual leadership in two dramatic and significant ways. The pastor has become first a leader of community prayer and worship and, second, a promoter of renewed spirituality.

The immediate and most demanding challenge of Vatican II was the renewal of liturgical prayer and worship. The pastor was called to lead the community to participation in worship, to new and more active roles in liturgical celebrations, and to a dynamic style of public prayer. Perhaps even more demanding than leading the people to a renewed sense of celebration, pastors found that

---

3. The most recent expression of the fundamental functions can be found in the revised *Code of Canon Law,* cc. 528, 529, 530.

they, like all priests, had to change and modify their own personal style of public worship leadership.

Since pastors had primary responsibility for the administration and physical plant of the parish, to them also fell the task of changing the physical setting of worship. Sanctuaries were redesigned, altars repositioned, and communion rails removed. Since reaction to these changes come immediately and forcefully, pastors came to understand how much the physical appearance and symbols of religious experience meant to their people. Initially, good liturgical practice often clashed with the taste and religious sentiments of many of the people.

There has been a gradual maturing process in parish liturgical life. With the passage of time, much of the experimentation led to a new, vibrant genre of worship and created enthusiasm about liturgical prayer. Most pastors are now more comfortable in the role of leader of worship. The people, by and large, have affirmed the relevance of the liturgical renewal, and they remain genuinely enthusiastic about their roles and their increased participation.

As the renewal of Vatican II deepened, many pastors felt themselves called to invite their parish communities to a more profound spiritual renewal. The currents of spiritual renewal in the Church in the United States were many and varied. The solid tradition of personal prayer and Sunday worship were the foundations upon which newer spiritual movements were built. The Cursillo movement, charismatic renewal, Marriage Encounter, the rediscovery of meditation and spiritual direction, prayer and scripture study groups began to flourish, often in parish settings.

Parish programs emphasizing spiritual dimensions of renewal became the later part of the Vatican II experience. Processes such as RENEW, "Christ Renews His Parish," and the RCIA required the leadership and the intense participation of pastors in the experience. Requests for spiritual direction increased, often as a direct result of participation in renewal programs.

One very distinctive development in this regard was the emergence of diverse spiritualities that had their roots in cultural and ethnic heritages. The large and significant Hispanic communities in the United States had the freedom to develop more indigenous forms of prayer and liturgical worship. Black communities defined and created distinct forms of black worship and prayer. More recently, native Americans, new immigrants from Asia, and other racial and ethnic groups have multiplied and deepened this diversity. Their pastors learned that they were called to steep themselves in the traditions, culture, and language of the communities in which they were serving.

### b. Community Leadership

The pastor's task is not limited to individual care of the faithful. It extends by right also to the formation of a genuine Christian community.[4]

The formation and animation of community life have become increasingly identified as one of the central roles of the pastor in the parish. With demographic shifts and new patterns, many parishes in the United States could no longer automatically assume that there was a close-knit neighborhood community present. The task of developing a sense of belonging, a common sense of purpose, vision, and pride of membership had to be vigorously pursued.

The pastor in this enterprise of community building had several expectations made of him. He was expected to give explicit and personal leadership to important community projects within the parish. He was even expected to be present at all meetings of the parish, if only for the purpose of encouraging parish societies and groups.

He was not solely responsible for development of community. He was also called upon to develop the quality of community leadership in others. His task of community building was not one that he always exercised in a directive way, but one that occasionally called him to be facilitator and enabler. This image of the pastor as encouraging and enabling assumed a central place in the post-Vatican II era, even if, at times, such was not practiced fully.

He was called upon increasingly to exercise community leadership in the wider neighborhood and geographic community. Beginning in the late 1960s and early 1970s, many pastors exercised this role of neighborhood leadership in vigorous and forthright ways. A growing number of parishes became involved in aggressive community organizing on behalf of the poor, the disenfranchised, and the unrepresented. Some pastors were actively involved in disputes over segregation, open housing, and other social issues.

---

4. Second Vatican Council, *Decree on the Ministry and Life of Priests,* no. 6.

8

Their parishes often became the focal point for this kind of organizing activity.

This call to the pastor to be countercultural and prophetic has prevailed over the years. In recent times, it has been given renewed emphasis because of the pastoral statements of the American bishops on war and peace and the justice dimensions of the American economy.

Closely related to this neighborhood community leadership role was the pastor's growing association with ecumenical and interfaith groups. One of the immediate results of Vatican II's appreciation for other churches was a great flurry of ecumenical activity. The discovery of profound similarities among the Christian religions especially led ministers and priests in a particular locality to shared prayer. Frequently, community action was interreligious in scope, and experience taught that the most effective community action was that which was ecumenical and broad-based.

c. Administrative Leadership

Even before Vatican II, the administrative complexity of parishes could vary, especially in relation to the size and location of the parish. Since Vatican II, the pastor's administrative responsibilities and staff leadership requirements have multiplied to the degree that even relatively small parishes require technical and organizational leadership skills that are often very sophisticated.

Nowhere was this form of leadership more relevant than in those circumstances where the pastor was working with and developing the collegial structures of the parish, especially the parish or pastoral council. Many pastors readily admit the difficulties they experienced in forming and organizing parish councils. They soon learned, however, that these participative structures demanded time and skill to make them effective and productive. Parish councils could be cohesive, effective working groups, or they could be groups of people searching for their identity and a clear scope of responsibilities.

It would, thus, be naive to infer that all experiences of collegial parish administration were positive. In a situation without time-tested models or patterns, there were bound to be many mistakes. While many pastors had a deep commitment to collegial ministry, they lacked the skills or astuteness that only experience and training bring. In spite of the experimental nature of much parish council activity, many pastors have discovered that they were useful, forceful, and effective means of engaging the gifts of the people of the parish community in meeting the needs of the entire parish.

As activities expanded and forms of ministry diversified, parishes began to take on an administrative complexity heretofore not present. Even the simple organizational problems of scheduling and space usage became complex. Most pastors learned to plan meetings and to structure them carefully and productively. Expectations upon pastors to conform to standards and regulations increased dramatically. Diocesan regulations multiplied as some dioceses standardized accounting procedures for parishes and demanded annual or even monthly reports that asked for very detailed information. Regulations were also issued by building commissions, liturgical commissions, and catechetical commissions.

In addition to the regulations generated by church agencies, state and local regulations complicated the administrative life in parishes and of pastors. Zoning ordinances, health and safety regulations, and fire codes were just some of the standards with which pastors had to comply. It is safe to assert that these expectations and demands often had a negative effect on many a pastor.

While some found that they had a natural flair for administration, many have indicated that it is parish administration that gives them the least satisfaction, not only because it is the area in which they feel least skilled, but also because it seems alien to the exercise of priestly ministry. Some set themselves to the task of learning administrative skills while others, with the flexibility and resources to do so, began to employ lay men and women as parish administrators, relieving themselves of the growing administrative burden.

## 2. Teaching

Teaching and proclaiming the kingdom are integral functions of all Christians, but they are even more an explicit and pointed responsibility of the pastor.[5]

---

5. The revised *Code of Canon Law,* c. 528,1 is even more detailed in its exposition of this responsibility for the pastor. He is to instruct the faithful especially through the homily and through catechetical formation. He is to promote social justice, care for the Catholic education of children, and bring the gospel message to those who have ceased practicing religion.

Before Vatican II, teaching the adults of the parish was accomplished through preaching from the pulpit and, to a lesser degree, through adult discussion groups. The teaching of young people was delegated to the sisters and brothers in parochial school or the growing CCD movement. After Vatican II, the responsibility for teaching and the teaching role of the pastor emerged in new and significant ways.

The first challenge for pastors was to learn what the conciliar documents taught and then structure methods and opportunities to communicate that message to their people. This task was complicated by the continuing stream of implementation documents, decrees and directives that followed the close of the Council.

What emerged were two levels of responsibility in this role of the pastor: to be teacher and supervisor of teachers; and to ensure that teaching was done.

Opportunities for direct teaching were numerous—classes, lectures, retreats—but the central opportunity was the Sunday homily. Like all priests, pastors had to adopt a new method of preaching based on the Scriptures and in the homily style. Some returned to school and tried to learn the new cadence and content of homiletic style.[6] They rethought the central role of the homily in worship and even redesigned sanctuaries to emphasize the importance of the Word and its proclamation.

Pastors have never had a reputation for being timid about speaking their mind but the post-Council years saw the increase in the need to speak the Church's mind on several controversial subjects. The national policy debates on racism, discrimination, the right of workers to organize, the right to life, war and peace, and a host of local social issues brought into sharp focus the responsibility of the pastor to be a prophetic voice in the community. While such responsibility was not always fulfilled, when it was, his message was not always welcome. Consequently, some pastors suffered isolation, rejection, and, on occasion, even threats. Although some of these national policy questions have receded in public interest, the prophetic voice of many a pastor continues to be heard on fundamental pro-life issues, war and peace, and economic rights.

---

6. For treatment of this subject, see NCCB Committee on Priestly Life and Ministry, *Fulfilled in Your Hearing: The Homily in the Sunday Assembly* (Washington, D.C.: USCC Office of Publishing and Promotion Services, 1982).

In addition to teaching directly, the pastor had the responsibility of organizing or reorganizing the entire teaching mission of the parish. Initially, he had to understand the new methodologies and content of the catechetical movement and even familiarize himself with the debate over content versus method. While he was learning the language and technique, he also had to organize the recruitment, training, and often the supervision of the volunteer lay teachers. In the medium-sized and larger parishes, directors of religious education were employed and financial resources were allocated to support the rapidly expanding education programs.

The second phase of religious education renewal occurred as many parish leaders began to sense the urgent need for training and formation experiences for adults. There was a shift from exclusively child-oriented programs to a full range of those geared to people of different ages and stages of religious formation. Lecture series, seminars, discussion groups, and eventually sacramental preparation programs became part of most parish programs. Especially in the area of sacramental formation, most pastors came to see the intimate connection between catechetics and celebration. This underscored the need for strong collaboration between pastors and religious education specialists.

In many circumstances, as the ministry of religious education was struggling to establish itself, some pastors found that they had to mediate disputes that cropped up around this program. Religious education directors complained about the parish willingness to subsidize schools and the reluctance to fund religious education. Parents who had been raised on the Baltimore Catechism became alarmed when they felt that their children were not given the traditional teaching of the Church.

Another major adjustment for many pastors was their increasing dependence on the religious education specialist. Many of the religious and laity who entered this ministry had attained graduate degrees in the field. The pastors, on the other hand, struggled with their responsibility to be the primary teachers of the truths of the faith and the corresponding reality that a growing number of laity and religious were better trained in current catechetical methods than they were. Some pastors also found, to their chagrin, that the multiplication of these religious education ministries, which were originally intended to relieve them of responsibilities, were at times generating more work and attention.

Dramatic changes were also occurring in the parochial school system. Pastors found that they had to respond to a set of circumstances caused not so much by the renewal of Vatican II but by economic, demographic, and personnel realities that were beyond their control. The number of women and men religious available for teaching in schools was declining. This was due, in great part, to a falling off of vocations as well to the fact that many chose to enter ministries other than teaching. Lay teachers had to be employed in their place. As salaries for lay teachers were greater, and as religious began to receive more realistic stipends, the costs of education rose dramatically. In many urban areas, the percentage of non-Catholic children attending the Catholic school increased as Catholic schools became a viable alternate to public education.

While most pastors and principals generally worked in harmony, there was occasional conflict in facing decisions about the mission of the school, the parish financial subsidy, and even the very existence of the school program itself. Parents became much more directly engaged in school programs as home-school associations and boards of education formed and became active in fund raising, policy decisions, and other activities. Some parents became staunch advocates for the continuation of the school program. The decision to close a school, faced by many pastors, was always a painful experience. The teaching ministry of the pastor, then, did not become less central to his role, but it did become a more diversified and more specialized one. It also became a function that could be delegated to competent professionals.

## 3. Pastoral Care

Pastoral care—responding to those most in need—remains at the heart of the role of the pastor. However, this function also developed some unique expressions.

What came into clearer focus for pastors during the period of renewal was the perceived connection between the sacramental life of the parish and the normal life cycle of families and the community. The sacramental celebrations of birth, death, marriage, maturity, and illness were opportunities for pastoral care and spiritual enrichment that had no parallel. In reality, the sacraments are encounters with the Lord and have always been so. The renewal, however, encouraged pastors to make the celebration of these spiritual rites more meaningful events in the lives of their people.

The American parish tradition of priests and pastors who are close to their people and their needs remained strong. Because of dramatic social and demographic changes, however, the pastoral needs of parish communities were changing also. The homebound, the handicapped, and the elderly increased in number and required a special pastoral response in every parish community. The number of ethnic and cultural minorities grew, especially in more recent years, and many parishes were not only bilingual and bicultural but multilingual and multicultural. In primarily Hispanic communities, the Catholic tradition found itself challenged by an aggressive evangelization effort by fundamentalist churches.

Even the traditional pastoral needs of parishes were shaping themselves in different and unique ways. Family life and the pressures that it experienced in contemporary society led bishops and pastors to place special emphasis on the needs of families. The number of broken marriages was increasing, as was the number of single-parent families. Pastors found that they needed the skills of marriage counseling, the ability to listen and to give insight and not just instruction. The number of widowed, separated, and divorced people grew, as did the number of single and married young professional people in the parish.

It soon became evident that the particular and unique needs of the local community were the measures that pastors used to determine the shape of their pastoral response. Many examples could be cited. One of the great monuments to the genuine pastoral sense of the Church in large cities was the decision to stay with the poor in the city as populations shifted to urban areas. Old urban parishes with large plants had few people, but they maintained a strong will to survive. In the southwestern and western sections of the United States, the outreach to the migrant worker and the undocumented became a very special form of pastoral care and sensitivity. More recently, in the midwest, the rural poor and the farmer were the focus of intense pastoral concern. Many pastors in the midwestern industrial belt were concerned about the unemployment of their parishioners, while many in the South were assisting their people to organize and seek representation in the workplace.

All through these years, the Catholic population was experiencing a great diversification. It was no longer mainly a working class, ethnic population. It encompassed the poorest as well as the very prosperous. This diversity placed serious demands on pastors to expand their horizons, and this, in turn, made the ministry of pastor very complex. A pastor might find himself in one assignment ministering to the urban poor and, within a few short years, he might be asked to serve in a wealthy suburban community. The

14

ability to respond to such a wide variety of local needs is witness to the flexibility and sensitivity that have become the hallmarks of the contemporary American pastor.

## A Specialized Ministry

In reviewing this brief summary of the changing role that they helped to create, pastors should experience a well-deserved sense of satisfaction. While far from perfect or ideal, the transformed role of pastor has met the demands of contemporary pastoral theology as well as the needs of the American people. It combines the qualities of inspiration, collaboration, sensitivity, and organization that are particularly fitted to the American parish community.

This historical review has led the Committee on Priestly Life and Ministry to conclude that the contemporary pastorate has become a "specialized ministry." Because of the unique demands made on the pastor, because of the variety and the cluster of skills required to do this ministry effectively, the pastorate is not just a generic priestly function.

Two implications follow from this conclusion. First, the pastorate is a ministry that must be learned and mastered. It requires a series of skills and competencies that can be identified and taught. Focused theological training, collaborative skills and techniques, and fundamental principles of organization and administration are only some of the requirements for effective pastoring. (Methods for pastor formation and preparation will be discussed later in this paper.)

Second, not all priests have the ability or the desire to exercise pastoral leadership as pastors. The role of the priest and the role of the pastor, while overlapping, are not the same. Becoming a pastor should not be automatic or be an assumed "promotion." It certainly should not be simply viewed as a reward for years of service.

## B. Changing Relationships

One of the major shifts in the lives of pastors since Vatican II can be seen in the way that they related to bishops, to fellow priests, and to parishioners. The quality, style, and intensity of relationships—all of these have undergone significant change and modification, often with some difficulty, as a result of the renewal experience.

## 1. With Bishops

The relationship of a pastor to a bishop has always been a rich and symbolic bond, beginning with the day of the priest's ordination. Like all priests, pastors are appointed directly by the diocesan bishop. They have traditionally felt a strong sense of accountability to the bishop himself. The strength of this bond did not diminish in the years since the Council, even with the enhanced role of auxiliary bishops, the establishment of vicars for clergy, and personnel boards. Pastors are conscious that, if anything goes wrong, they are the ones who are held accountable for the conduct of the parish community entrusted to their care. Therefore, they continue to feel the need of direct access to the diocesan bishop, and many bishops insist that this be their policy.

The changes in the relationship between pastors and bishops can be found not so much in the strength of the bond between them but in the manner and the structures through which they relate. Consequently, the relationship between bishops and pastors took a more personal turn. Many bishops came to see themselves as brothers to their priests, as fellow pastors. The Second Vatican Council urged this personal bond between priests and bishops when it said, "On account of this common sharing in the same priesthood and ministry then, bishops are to regard their priests as brothers and friends and are to take the greatest interest they are capable of in their welfare, both temporal and spiritual."[7]

This new sense of relationship became institutionalized in many dioceses through structures that brought bishops into more frequent contact with pastors. Parish visitations on a regular basis became a method for many bishops to get a firmer sense of the needs of individual pastors in parish communities. Priest councils/senates broke new ground in bringing the ideas and concerns of priests and pastors to the attention of the bishop in a formal manner. The sacramental bonding of the diocesan bishop with the presbyterate is exemplified best with the canonical requirement of the

---

7. Second Vatican Council, *Decree on the Ministry and Life of Priests*, no. 7.

presbyteral council. Within this structure, the wisdom of pastors is articulated for the overall good governance of the diocese.

While some of the new structures tended to facilitate the communication between bishops and pastors, other structures were perceived by pastors as creating layers of bureaucracy that separated them from direct access to the bishop. Many pastors felt excluded from personal access to their bishop when they had to relate to such entities as clergy personnel boards, building commissions, school and religious education offices, and liturgical commissions. They frequently complained—and still do—that the flood of programs, policies, structures, guidelines, and mail that originated from these bodies simply created more red tape and obstacles to their direct communication and relationship with the bishop.

It is clear, then, that there have been two almost contradictory trends in the relationship between bishops and pastors since Vatican II. The first is a series of trends that broke down old barriers between priests and bishops and established a more direct, more intimate, and more personal style of relationship. On the other hand, there was a series of trends that created new obstacles and made the relationship of pastors and bishops more distant. The latter may explain the sentiment expressed by some pastors that the complexity of their roles is not fully appreciated by those in authority. It is evident that not all obstacles to mutual and improved communication have been removed.

## 2. With Parishioners

Since 1965, the Church has not only undergone changes encouraged by the teachings of the Second Vatican Council, but it has also witnessed strong cultural and social changes as well. One of the strongest trends in these years was the change occurring within the Catholic community itself. It began to move from being a predominantly ethnic and working-class community to a more educated, middle-class, and professional one. Additionally, the same years saw a rapid growth in new ethnic, racial, and cultural diversity within the Catholic Church.

Besides the inevitable changes that education, greater wealth, and ethnic diversity were producing, the late 1960s and early 1970s saw a mood of assertiveness among the people of this country. It was not just within the Catholic Church, of course, but the mood certainly affected the people in parishes throughout the United States. They, like their secular counterparts, were demanding rights

17

and asking to share in the authority and decision-making structures of the parish community.

Another cultural reality, more directly related to the internal work and life of parish communities themselves, was the growing volunteer ministry movements within the Catholic parishes of the United States. The lay apostolate and its call to live one's religious commitment actively began before Vatican II. Lay apostolate movements of the 1950s and early 1960s, such as the Christian Family Movement, the Cursillo, and the Young Christian Workers, created a readiness among Catholic people for more involvement as Christians in secular life and as Catholics in church life.

The invitation of the Second Vatican Council to live out baptismal and confirmation commitments as adult Christians called forth many thousands of people desiring to partake in the ministerial life of their parishes in new and active ways. The old sodalities and fraternal groups gave way to, or were joined by, organizations of volunteers more directly involved in ministerial roles.

Parents became more active in schools—on boards of education, in home-school associations, as aides or administrative assistants. As the liturgical renewal grew, there were many and varied liturgical ministries opened to lay persons that had never been available before ( e.g., lectors, eucharistic ministers, leaders of song, liturgical committee membership, etc.). In addition to their involvement in liturgical renewal, many people felt called in various ways to service of the poor and to the social ministry of the Church.

What is distinctive about this level of increasing involvement of lay persons is that many of the people who are engaged in these ministries received some form of training in this volunteer ministry before they undertook responsibilities at the parish level. Hundreds of diocesan and regional training programs and centers have been established. The increasingly well-trained volunteers also have become the group from which full-time lay ministers began to emerge.

Increased ministerial activity and broader decision-making involvement inevitably shaped the relationship of pastors with their people. The first obvious change was on the level of expectation that people had in relationship to pastors and the parish services and programs that would be provided. As people became more theologically and psychologically sophisticated, they expected more from their parish and from pastoral leadership. They wanted good administration, creative and meaningful prayer experiences, good homilies, and they expected pastors to respond in effective and personal ways to their needs. Pastors universally acknowledged

18

that the expectations of their people had risen dramatically in the past ten to fifteen years.

In addition to higher expectations, people became freer in the expression of their personal points of view and their complaints about the quality or shape of parish life. Frequently, pastors felt themselves caught between conflicting expectations of groups within the parish community. Many pastors still feel that most consultative groups have not relieved them of their responsibilities as much as adding another duty to their schedule.

One striking facet of the relationship of pastors to people was its style. People began to expect a more sensitive personal response. Pastors have traditionally maintained a sense of closeness to their people and, in a positive sense, many of the artificial and formal barriers of the past were removed. An even greater freedom of relationship emerged between pastor and people from the shared experiences of working for parish renewal.

### 3. With Priests, Deacons, and Lay Ministers

Among all of the changed relationships experienced by pastors, perhaps the most noticeable change was in the relationship between a pastor and the members of the parish staff.

Many priests who had become pastors before or during the Second Vatican Council had themselves suffered under authoritarian pastors, men whose power was unquestioned and whose decisions were unchallenged. When expressions such as "shared authority" and "participative decision making" came into practice, the post-Vatican II pastors could not help but feel a sense of resentment.

In spite of these early negative experiences, most pastors began to experiment with the application of the principles of collaboration and shared ministry. In some definitions of team ministry, all of the priests of the parish staff were to share equally in the ministerial decision-making life of the parish. Some dioceses implemented this understanding of shared priestly ministry in a very systematic fashion.[8]

Another parallel development has been the definition of team in a broader, more informal sense. A team would include all full-time or even part-time professional ministerial staff persons. Team

---

8. The Archdiocese of Hartford, Connecticut, for example.

ministry could mean coordinated and collaborative activities, or it could mean shared decision making. While there is no one standard or style of team ministry, this mode of collaborative ministry seems to be emerging as very common in parishes throughout the United States. For the most part, it has indeed proven to be a very workable model. Such shared ministries include regularly scheduled staff meetings, clear designation of pastoral duties, shared planning, and coordination of calendars. The pastor in this setting frequently acts as convener, leader, and director of the parish team. In a team setting, pastors frequently engage in staff development. They see to it that their staff members are relating effectively with each other and that they are growing in their ministerial and professional competence. Some parish teams spend a substantial amount of time in seminars and other developmental experiences, testing out their relationships, studying their preferred style of relating, and working out more effective means of communication. More and more, the need to "minister to the ministers" and to coordinate the gifts of all ministers is becoming a constitutive part of the role of the pastor.

In addition to the new relationships created by team or shared ministries, pastors discovered that they needed to adjust their manner of relating to individuals on the parish staffs.

Associate pastors (parochial vicars) created special demands on the pastor. In the early days after Vatican II, the relationships between pastors and associates were often divisive and difficult. There was deep friction over the meaning of change and renewal. Serious divisions in parish communities often became symbolized by pastors and associates who could not work together.

At the same time, many older and younger priests struggled to bridge the gap of misunderstanding that separated them. While frictions often developed, for most the process, understanding, sensitivity, and respect deepened on both sides. More significantly for the role of pastor, that period saw the emergence of the function of the "curate" from a clearly subordinate position to that of "associate" or "parochial vicar," a position that shares more directly in the pastor's responsibility and mission. It is a position of co-worker, but still under the authority of the pastor.[9] It may be said that, in the area of collegial effort, a great many pastors have been enablers of young priests while allowing themselves to be challenged by the young priests' views.

---

9. Cf. *Code of Canon Law,* cc.545-555.

The more recent experience of pastors, many of whom were associates in the early days of renewal, has been that the demands and needs of younger clergy have changed. Some priest associates practice less confrontation, while others are more likely to request a strong relational and tension-free atmosphere in the working out of parish life and the ministry. There is, however, a popular perception that a new ideological split exists between pastors and associates. In many cases, more recently ordained associates are often perceived as more conservative and supportive of traditional modes of parish ministry.[10]

The emergence of lay ministers and the restoration of the permanent deacons (full-time and part-time) as active members of parish staffs also addressed the special sensitivity needed by all parties. A dimension of lay experience, especially the experience of married and family life, began to enrich parish services. At the same time, lay ministers and permanent deacons struggled for identity and their proper place in parish life. This was particularly true of the permanent diaconate.

The diaconate was first situated in the midst of liturgical reform, as was the ministry of the laity. They both served as liturgical ministers, as readers and ministers of the Eucharist. The experience of these new forms of ministry in the beginning of this liturgical reform was bound to be accompanied by some tension.

In this context, it must be noted that the diaconate is a lifetime commitment to ministry and the orientation of each formation program is toward a ministry of service (i.e., the formation of men who were to be sacramental signs of the presence of the servant Jesus). The fact that the vast majority of deacons were married men with families, some of them still young, was bound to raise a number of questions as to who the deacon was for the life of the Church. The temptation, at times, was to measure the deacon's contribution to ministry by what he did. What was most obvious to the parish community was the liturgical ministry of the deacon

---

10. This perception has been found to have some basis in fact. See *Attitudes of American Priests in 1970 and 1985 on the Church and Priesthood,* a recently completed survey of clergy attitudes conducted by Dean Hoge, Joseph J. Shields and Mary Jeanne Verdieck (Washington, D.C.: The Catholic University of America, March 1986).

at the Sunday celebration; few were witnesses to his day-in, day-out ministry of service.[11]

The introduction of the permanent deacon, like so many of the reforms that preceded him, was often with minimal or no catechesis. As a result, there was bound to be confusion, not least among the pastors with whom the deacon was to minister. Consequently, with the advent of lay ministers, many of whom are equipped with advanced degrees in their specialties, the perception is sometimes taken that permanent deacons are superfluous. It is evident, however, that many lay ministers are also finding integration within long-erected diocesan and parish structures no easier. It is often a slow process.

While it will probably take at least another generation to work at these processes of acceptance and integration, what is increasingly evident are the ever more numerous needs for which ministers—deacon and lay—will be required.

Another of the more sensitive areas of change in relationship style is with women staff members, both religious and lay. Catholic parishes in the United States exist within the framework of the larger cultural context of the women's movement, and they are touched directly by these experiences. In this regard, women wish and deserve to make equal contributions along with their male counterparts.

Many pastors have found that their relationship with women religious has changed significantly on the personal and ministerial level. While fewer women religious were available for the ministry of Catholic education, a growing number were filling ministerial roles such as pastoral assistants, directors of religious education, parish administrators, and the like.

Communities of women religious expended enormous energy in renewal and in changing the structures of religious life. These changes have not always been understood, respected, or, at times, adequately communicated to pastors. Many sisters who came into pastoral life brought high expectations of shared responsibility. Because of the continued ambiguity about the roles of pastor and associate pastor, these expectations were not always realized; many

---

11. For further information on the permanent diaconate see NCCB Committee on the Permanent Diaconate, *Permanent Deacons in the United States: Guidelines on Their Formation and Ministry,* revised edition (Washington, D.C.: USCC Office of Publishing and Promotion Services, 1985).

tasks and responsibilities were not assigned on the basis of pastoral competencies. Despite misunderstandings and frustration, mutual respect and learning continues to grow between pastors and women religious as these women play an even more central role in parish life.

Relationships with women, both religious and lay, changed in more fundamental ways. A set of values and ideas that promoted human growth became part of the expectation placed upon pastors. All priests were encouraged to be more fully human, especially to be more spontaneous persons and less stilted in their relationships with women. In addition, pastors especially were asked to respond not only to the perception but to the reality of discrimination against women in society and more so within church structures. These questions took on more than theoretical significance as many pastors realized that what was required of them was a higher degree of psychosexual maturity than was required in a more protected atmosphere of separation from women.

Collaboration

What typifies the transformation in the relationships of pastors more than anything is the word *collaboration*. Relationships with bishops, people, and staff have become more mutual in character, more open to equal exchange of ideas. Simply stating that fact does not capture the long hours of discussion and experiment that pastors have invested in creating new collaborative structures and experiences. There were legitimate questions about the loss of authority, effectiveness in leadership, and even about pastoral efficiency. But, the experience has also discovered the deep scriptural and pastoral roots of the notion of collaboration. St. Paul was explicit in his letters about the need to develop "a unity in the work of service building up the Body of Christ" (Eph 4:12). He affirmed that all were given different gifts by the Holy Spirit, that there were all sorts of different service to be done. He provided the model of the Body of Christ—the organic interplay of interdependent parts— as the model for cooperation (1 Cor 12:4-30). This form of scripturally based pastoral collaboration has required certain personal characteristics in pastors: receptivity, openness, recognition of others' giftedness, and the "pastoral love" so evident in the writings of St. Paul. It has demanded, too, a high degree of personal security.

The transition from a model where the pastor was responsible for everything to a model of shared ministry is still in process but the direction is clear. While the phrase "coordinator of charisms" is not very poetic, it does have the virtue of stating explicitly what has become a dominant and necessary role for pastors in today's Church.

## C. A Changing Environment

Because it is a survey of national experience, this document must generalize about parish life and the role of the pastor. It is important to note, however, that there are significant differences among the parishes in this country and, therefore, in the role of the pastor. In addition to the preferred style of the individual pastor himself, one of the most important differences between parishes is the environment in which they are set. A systematic look at some environmental factors will illustrate how these factors determine the role and responsibility of the ministry of pastor.

### 1. The Parish

The setting of the individual parish community creates the distinctive features of that parish's life and, therefore, the role of its pastor. Geographic size and location, social and cultural context, ethnic and racial composition, as well as long years of another pastor's style or the struggle to maintain schools are environmental factors that have made their impact on many parishes.

It would be impossible to discuss all of the combinations of these factors and their influence on the role of the pastor. It might be useful, however, to point to one factor that has, more than many others, changed the environment of parishes and the demands on pastoral leadership—migration. The out-migration of peoples from the cities has created inner-city parishes and the sprawl of suburban parishes; the migration of millions of Hispanics into the United States from Mexico, Puerto Rico, Cuba, Central and South America has created hundreds of Spanish-speaking, bilingual and multicultural parishes.

Recent arrivals include Haitians, Koreans, Vietnamese, Laotians, and a large number of Poles. The shift of a large number of Catholics from the Northeast and Midwest to the South and Southwest will likely continue in the next decade and dramatically reshape parish populations.

24

This factor of migration, in combination with those listed earlier, only heightened the diversity among parishes, even those within the same diocese. Not all parishes and, therefore, not all pastorates are exactly the same. What works well in one setting or environment will not necessarily work in another.

The environment of a parish sets limits on what is possible in a given community, as well as defining the potential of that community. Hence, experienced pastors who moved from assignment to assignment knew that it was very important to give themselves transitional time, time to learn the reality and the uniqueness of any given parish situation. Many have learned also that the creation and formulation of a distinctive mission statement for each parish was one method of capturing and responding to the uniqueness of each community.

Another implication of the environmental differences among parishes is the difficulty experienced by pastors who came from a culture or ethnic background different from the one to which they were assigned. The experience of the Anglo priest in Hispanic communities; the black pastor in a white suburban community; priests from other nations; or a priest from a working-class family who must pastor in an affluent community—all realized the significant adjustment that a changed environment places on them.

The consequence of these identifiable differences among parishes led dioceses to consider carefully the question of assignment and reassignment of pastors. Personnel boards in many dioceses attempted to identify significant differences and the real nature of the demands of a particular parish community. Personnel boards did not have an infinite supply of priests to select from and did not always function effectively, but their avowed purpose was to select the most qualified priest for each assignment. They attempted to communicate significant factors to priests who were about to be assigned as pastor.

## 2. The Diocese

Every parish is part of a larger local Church: a diocese or archdiocese. The life of the parish and the role of the pastor are conditioned, to some extent, by the setting the diocese creates through its structures, policies, and programs.

As noted earlier, pastors commented repeatedly about the expansion of central diocesan administrative structures since Vatican II. For the pastor, this has been a mixed blessing. It created a whole new series of demands on his time, but it also has changed his role in several other ways.

Most diocesan offices attempted to keep pastors better informed through regular written communications. The creation of the positions of vicar and dean forged a closer link between the pastor and the diocese. In many dioceses, pastors had a voice in the creation of diocesan policy and were usually consulted about assignments of priests to their parish and about their own assignments. While diocesan commissions and offices did generate extra work, they have also served as effective supports and technical advisors, where they were operating efficiently.

Where there was effective interaction between parishes and diocesan central administration, most pastors moved more closely into the mainstream of diocesan life. They tended to suffer less from *parochialism*—what one pastor called "the subtle drug" of the pastor.

### 3. The Universal Church

Decisions made in the Holy See can become a central concern of the pastor in the local and individual parish. In a sense, this entire reflection is a description of the impact the universal Church has had on the role of pastor since the Second Vatican Council. The influence and impact of the universal Church on the local parish is continual. Just two recent examples might be cited.

The promulgation of the revised Code of Canon Law is beginning to have a substantial impact on parish life. Canonists are still in the process of determining the exact effect of the revised legislation on the parish and diocese. Parish communities are also exploring, in practical ways, the implications made by the revised Code on the role of the pastor, staffing of parishes, financial administration, and other areas.

A second example is the Extraordinary Synod completed in 1985. The results of that Synod will no doubt offer some future guidance to pastors about the ongoing implementation of Council teaching at the parish level. While the basic teachings of the Council were reaffirmed, certain areas of church life were cited as needing revision.

What these two examples illustrate is the swiftness of modern communications, which makes the process of implementation of policies from the Holy See very immediate and very direct on the local parish and pastor. Swiftness of communication, however, does not ensure immediate compliance or automatic internalization of all the teachings or policy decisions of the various Roman Congregations. It can be said that the great majority of pastors in the United States take very seriously their responsibility to implement, on the parish level, the teaching and directives of the pope, the curia, and international synods. They find, in general, that their parishioners are willing to do the same. They have, however, encountered serious resistance among their people to particular areas of teaching and pastoral discipline. The social teaching of the Church in the areas of war and peace, nuclear arms, workers' rights, and racism has not always received a positive response from parishioners. Others either challenge or ignore the teaching of the Church on birth control and sexual ethics.

In an American society that is actively changing its attitudes and structures with regard to the role of women, the restrictions upon women's service to the Church seem out of character in a typical American parish. The resulting struggle between fidelity to the teaching of the Church and personal integrity, between freedom of conscience and the responsibility to conform to legitimate authority, is one that has become familiar to pastors.

## D. Changing Spirituality and Morale

To speak of a unique and distinctive "spirituality of the pastor" is to speak about a book yet to be written; for, as one pastor put it, "the ascetical theology of pastoring in today's Church is the most underdeveloped and needed theological reflection in the Church today."

While there has been no systematic development of a spirituality for the pastor, there exists a recurring theme in the comments of pastors about their own spiritual needs. They do express anxiety about being so preoccupied with administration or so consumed by responding to their people's needs that they neglect their own spiritual nourishment, ironically, out of a sense of duty.

Reflections from pastors about other aspects of their ministry do offer some clues to the spiritual sources of their own strength and patterns of spiritual development within the pastorate.

Many pastors have given witness to the power of the Word in their own ministry. As they have meditated more deeply on Scripture, as they have tried to interpret its meaning for their people,

27

they have inevitably found that the Word does inspire and touch them personally as they read and proclaim it daily.

The Eucharist is inevitably at the heart of all priestly spirituality. For the priest, Eucharist, prayer, and personal spirituality are meant to take on a heightened significance. Most pastors realize intensely that the Eucharist builds up the Church, that the source and zenith of the community's experiences are to be found in the celebration of the Eucharist. This celebration is not just the fulfillment of a duty or an obligation; it creates what is the goal of all Christian enterprise: unity in God through Christ.

The prayer of the pastor is often in communal settings. In addition to the celebration of the Eucharist, many pastors will regularly participate in shared prayer and days of recollection with staff. More and more pastors are praying the Liturgy of the Hours with parishioners or fellow priests and religious. A growing number have become more comfortable with spontaneous prayer with those in need or in counseling. These experiences often bring prayer beyond a purely individual discipline.

While common prayer contributes much to their spiritual growth, most pastors are also aware of the need for quiet prayer in their lives. In all probability, it is in such quiet time, often before the Blessed Sacrament, that many of the difficulties of ministry are better understood and solutions devised. The personal prayer of the priest is and continues to be the source and strength of his ministry.

The quality of pastors' spirituality also rises with their sharing the faith life of people, especially in those critical moments of sorrow and disappointment, of pain and death. These moments continue to make pastors deeply aware that Christ's love and consolation are the great need in their own lives as well as their people.

A word must be said here about a unique contribution to the spirituality of the priest/pastor. It is that of priest support-groups as found in many dioceses. Over the years, they have proved to be a source of spiritual awareness and growth for many. Through regular prayerful and fraternal association with their brothers in the priesthood, many pastors have found the strength and courage so needed in the exercise of their ministry.

All told, it would be a matter of pure conjecture to discuss patterns of ascetical practice among pastors with this one exception: the manner in which many pastors accept the difficulties of their changing ministry. The tensions of the office and, in some cases, the declining prestige are accepted by many as the unique asceticism of the pastor. What would otherwise be only a matter of personal discomfort or dissatisfaction is often raised to the level of spiritual significance by patient acceptance.

In a time of radical change or transition, personal stress is inevitable and is, indeed, part of the productive chemistry of change. The effect of the transformation of the pastorate on the morale of priests has been a matter of active concern for many dioceses. A mixed picture emerges from closer study. The changing role of pastor caused deep pain and personal tension for many priests, while others found the atmosphere of change and transformation one of invigorating challenge to their creativity. The usual case was that the pastorate over the past twenty years has been a mixture of success and failure, joy and pain.

The innate goodness and responsiveness of people to the Word of God, their disarming hunger for things spiritual, their willingness to respond to the most needy among them are all sources of encouragement and wonder for pastors. The growing enthusiastic response to the vision of Vatican II created an energy of its own. One of the prized outcomes of renewal was the response of people to spiritual enrichment programs and the large number of parishioners who developed an active sense of ministry and willingness to be of service to others.

Many pastors found the new participative and collaborative style of parish life very compatible with their own ministerial goals. Developing staff members and the mutual nourishment that resulted were a special source of fulfillment. The interaction of clergy, religious, and lay women and men was a healthy and exciting experience for many pastors.

These reflections have emphasized the positive and productive experiences of the pastors during the renewal years. The full picture includes, of course, failures, deep pain and anxiety for many, decisions to leave the priesthood, as well as outright incompetence.

The main negative factors of morale identified by pastors often relate to superiors' and peoples' response, or lack of response, to their ministry. The unrealistic and even contrary expectations of people and bishops have created standards that pastors, try as they might, could not always live up to completely. Many pastors state that they often felt underappreciated and unacknowledged. In most dioceses, there was no consistent method of affirmation or reward for successful pastors or for parochial vicars.

The term *burnout* has become a cliche, but it does serve as an appropriate description of the phenomenon of intense and extensive exhaustion felt by many pastors. Such exhaustion may result from a particularly demanding assignment, an assignment where there has been substantial hostility from the people over issues such as liturgical renewal, social justice, or school tuition. The exhaustion may result from a situation where there has been a strong extended and debilitating power struggle between the pastor and his people. It has also risen from one's inability or refusal to take personal time for rest, prayer, and study. In summary, all these have contributed to a feeling of uncertainty and discouragement on the part of many pastors.

The problem of loneliness for the pastor is widespread. It is obvious in the small, one-priest parish that is separated by long distances from other priests. There is, however, a special kind of loneliness in a rectory with other priests when relationships with one another are poor.

In spite of morale problems and, perhaps, because of a developing spirituality, many pastors have consciously recommitted themselves to the priesthood as experienced in the pastorate. It is evident that being such a pastor can generate a new self-giving and a deeper commitment to the service of people.

At the same time, many associate pastors are also experiencing deeper commitment to their priesthood. While their position involves unique challenges, there is a growing sense of collaboration both with the pastor and with the people. They, too, have been encouraged to develop their ministerial skills and to recognize the very special value of their service to the Church. Such a commitment to priestly service, shared with the pastor, is a dimension of vocation that can become life-giving to the parish community and a source of personal fulfillment to those priests who serve it.

# III. The Forms and Styles of Pastoring

This brief sketch of the roles and relationships of the pastor could never begin to capture the depth of feelings that so many pastors share when talking about their ministry. Their feeling is exuberant when expressing the joys and satisfactions that come from being so critical to community life. Sometimes, that feeling is one of frustration at unachieved or unachievable goals. At other times, it is annoyance that anyone could ask such an obvious question as "What is your role?" At all times, the tone is authentic, sincere, and honest. Consequently, these pages have not attempted to capture the personal feelings and experiences of pastors as much as they have tried to describe their substantial accomplishment.

The majority of pastors over the past twenty years have fashioned new forms and new styles of pastoring. In the process of implementing the renewal called for by Vatican II, they have created not one but several different and, at times, overlapping types of pastoring.

It would be an overstatement to say that clearly distinct and separable types of pastoring have been the product of the renewal experience. It would not, however, be far from the truth to say that different pastors have consciously chosen different styles or a particular emphasis in their pastoral ministry. The differences may originate in the needs of the community or they may be the result of the personality, convictions, or training of the pastor himself.

The particular pastoral styles that have been developed will be worth noting since their identification and description might further the dialogue still in process on the appropriate position of the pastor and his still rapidly changing role. These realities give the opportunities for further reflection and discussion.

31

## A. The Pastor as Proclaimer of God's Word

This form of pastoring emphasizes the role of the pastor as preacher and teacher of God's Word, as leader of prayer and spiritual guide for the people. It situates the pastor primarily as the spiritual leader of the community. It stresses prayerful and reverent preparation of homilies, leadership of spiritual renewal programs, and the ability to provide spiritual guidance and direction.

On a more personal level, this style of pastoring situates the pastor as one formed by and deeply rooted in the Scriptures and growth in personal conversion. It attempts to model continual visible conversion in his own life as an example for his people.

## B. The Pastor as Leader of Worship

This form of pastoring situates and underscores his position as presider at Eucharist and chief liturgist of the parish community. It stresses his provision for the celebration of the liturgy as the source and summit of the life of the parish. Thus, careful planning, study, and training for the various ministers, as well as for the parish at large, are overseen by the pastor.

## C. The Pastor as Builder of the Community

The pastor as coordinator of the community's gifts, and as unifier and facilitator, identifies the various charisms within the parish. The now well-known image of "the orchestra leader" from *As One Who Serves*[12] gives concrete and explicit expression to this form of pastoral emphasis. In this context, he spends time discovering the talents of his staff and people. He forges links between individuals and groups, promotes consensus decision making, and prizes the establishment of collaboration and cooperation in all pastoral efforts.

---

12. NCCB Committee on Priestly Life and Ministry, *As One Who Serves: Reflections on the Pastoral Ministry of Priests in the United States* (Washington, D.C.: USCC Office of Publishing and Promotion Services, 1977), p. 46.

## D. The Pastor as Steward of the Community's Resources

The faithful stewardship of the community's resources is the focus of this style of pastoring. This is achieved through prudent administration, efficient organization of the various parish efforts or programs, and the provision of financial resources to carry out the parish mission. It emphasizes good order and good house-keeping. Such effective utilization of resources extends to the staff— the human resources of the parish. Here, tasks and responsibilities are clearly defined and coordinated. Parish policies and standards are articulated, and systems of communication and responsibilities are developed and utilized.

It will be obvious immediately that these dimensions of pastoring, in reality, constitute most of the possible functions of the pastor in today's—and tomorrow's—parish. The fact that they are diverse bears witness to the complexity of the role of the pastor. The fact that each demands a different set of skills is testament to the difficulty of the role.

This project was originally undertaken with the hope that it would offer some description of the role of pastor in today's Church. It has discovered that his role is still in the process of development and that it is very diverse.

What has been accomplished, however, has had a positive effect on the life of the Church in the United States. What is yet to be done will require much continuing support and understanding on the part of pastors and their people. It is hoped that this effort will lead to greater recognition of what has been achieved as well as a renewed commitment to assist pastors in their ever-changing and ever-challenging ministry.

# IV. Resources: A Pledge of Support

Pastors, as a group, seldom ask for or expect assistance in the performance of their duties. The history of the past twenty years, however, linked with the continuing demands of the future, have led dioceses, presbyteral councils, and pastor peer-groups to establish support systems for pastors on a diocesan and regional basis.

These developing and rapidly multiplying resources are described here so that they might provide models or starting points for those dioceses, regions, or pastor-groups that wish to pursue vigorously the establishment of a support network for pastors.

These reflections have led the Committee on Priestly Life and Ministry to the firm conclusion that active support for pastors is needed, deserved, and a responsibility of the whole Church. Active and well-resourced support systems speak louder than words of praise or affirmation. They are a concrete expression of esteem and concern and a tangible pledge of assistance to pastors. The support efforts that have been structured fall generally into three categories of those that support pastors: (1) in pastorate assignment and preparation; (2) during a pastorate assignment; and (3) at the time of transfer and retirement.

## A. Pastor Assignment and Preparation

The first and most obvious effort of bishops and clergy personnel boards is the careful selection of pastor assignments. Increasing care is being taken to describe and understand the unique characteristics and demands of a particular parish assignment and

35

to choose the most competent and qualified priest for that assignment. Compatibility with current parish structure, style, and pastoral philosophy is a critical ingredient of successful selection.

Even where there is no formal effort to prepare pastors for assignments, it is possible to assist prospective pastors by providing a clear and accurate description of the pastoral responsibilities they will be assuming. Giving an in-depth orientation to the needs of the parish and to the expectations of the bishop helps a pastor to set his own goals.

More formal courses of pastor preparation and pastor orientation have been developed. Many new-pastor or pastor-preparation courses are offered during the first months of a new assignment.

In some cases, course content focuses predominantly on administrative skills that range from fiscal and legal responsibilities to employer-employee relationships.[13] Since the most unfamiliar territory for many new pastors lies precisely in the details of financial and business administration, these workshops have been welcomed and well attended by many priests as they enter their first pastorate.

Other programs are more broadly focused in their content. Special attention is given to the challenges of community building and staff development.[14] Getting in touch with the parish history, developing parish vision and goals, and basic skills for effective meetings and conflict management, as well as parish and financial council development, are common features in a growing number of new-pastor courses.

These programs vary not only in content but also in length, structure, and style. In some dioceses, a single day at the chancery is offered to introduce the new pastor to financial procedures and the resources offered by various departments. In other cases, a week-long seminar is offered. In Region XI, a five-day workshop is followed by a self-designed project in the parish, and the program is concluded by another five-day session as participants come together to reflect on their pastorate "six months later."

A structured time and process for introduction has proved helpful not only for the first-time pastor but for those priests en-

---

13. For example, the seminar organized by the Texas Catholic Conference emphasizes these areas of skills training.

14. Pastor-training workshops in Region XI are organized around these areas of pastoral competence.

tering their second, third, or fourth assignments as pastor. The high level of interest and participation in new-pastor courses by experienced pastors underscores the distinctive needs of pastors in transition. The experience has proved rewarding for both new and old pastors alike. In response to the question of who will conduct these courses, the majority of pastors indicate that their preference is for experienced pastors not theoreticians or theologians.

## B. Support in Pastorate Assignment

Once a pastor has assumed a new assignment, and even in cases where there has been care in his preparation, efforts to sustain and underpin his ministry are still helpful.

As an extension of the pastor-preparation course, one diocese has initiated a "pastor mentor" program.[15] The "mentor" is an experienced pastor who will serve as counselor, friend, and guide to the newly appointed pastor. The competence and commitment of the mentor are key in the success of this structure but just as essential are formal structures of meeting and a preset agenda of issues to explore.

A growing number of dioceses have created the position of "regional vicar" or "dean." In many cases, a primary responsibility of the dean or vicar is to be directly supportive of the pastors of a particular region. These structures give the pastors access to someone in authority who can respond quickly, directly, and personally to their needs.

A more recent development in several dioceses has been the formation of spontaneous, self-help support-groups of pastors. The pastors in these groups come together in small numbers, usually to discuss common problems and to share experiences. In some cases, pastors will organize more formally to address issues that are pressing and important to them.

The "Convention of Pastors" is a continuing formation program developed by the National Organization for the Continuing Education of Roman Catholic Clergy (NOCERCC). These workshops, geared specifically to the needs of pastors, have been organized in

---

15. The Diocese of Rockville Centre, New York.

a number of areas in the country and are intended to help pastors develop their own unique pastoral skills.[16]

Over recent years, some dioceses and parishes have addressed the living conditions of their priests. Living in old, large, and expensive-to-maintain rectories (often without good housekeeping care) that combined living quarters with work quarters has had dire effects on many priests/pastors.

Some presbyteral councils have developed programs of alternate living situations. These, in most cases, have produced better conditions healthwise and ministrywise for pastors and parochial vicars.

Other methods of recognizing and affirming the good work of priests have also been an agenda item for many presbyteral councils, and several dioceses have experimented with honors dinners and awards ceremonies. Perhaps, the most appreciated form of recognition has been the extended sabbatical. Several programs in the United States and abroad offer ten-week to one-year courses in updating in theology, Scripture, and related pastoral topics.[17] Some dioceses allow the pastor to create his own sabbatical experience, offer partial or complete funding, and provide coverage at the parish during the pastor's absence.

Many pastors are seeking opportunities, on some regular basis, to review or assess their own ministry, and many dioceses have developed means for such review. Evaluation processes and ministry-review techniques are being used increasingly to assist pastors in assessing their own skills and in identifying areas of needed growth. These processes, in most cases, prove to be very supportive and demonstrate to pastors their real success and accomplishments.[18]

## C. Pastor Transfer and Retirement

The "term of office" policy for pastors has become a norm in many dioceses throughout the United States, and the National Con-

---

16. More information can be found in Appendix E.

17. Consult the National Organization for Continuing Education of the Roman Catholic Clergy, 5401 South Cornell Avenue, Chicago, IL 60615.

18. Among the dioceses that engage in regular ministerial review are Cleveland, Milwaukee, and others (see Appendices B, C, D).

ference of Catholic Bishops has, in conformity with the revised Code, established a National Norm for these policies.[19] This policy is intended to ensure regular and orderly change in parish assignments and has succeeded in preventing stagnation or inertia in many parishes. It is important, however, that transfer, especially under term of official statutes, not become an automatic move just for the sake of movement. Many priests have several assignments as pastors throughout the course of their ministry. Some clergy personnel boards and diocesan assignment offices are attempting to develop a pattern that gives a sense of progression to this series of assignments. In the attempt to vary assignments according to degree of difficulty or locality, personnel boards are trying to avoid the trap of assigning a priest as pastor to the same type of parish. Instead of repeating successes in similar assignments, pastors become exposed to new challenges and to opportunities for broadening their abilities within a wider range of pastoral needs.

One of the most difficult things for a priest to do is to resign or retire from the act of pastorate. No matter what a priest's age or even physical condition, he finds leaving his people a painful experience. There are ways of structuring the termination process in an honorable and dignified manner.[20] On occasion, even before the age of retirement, there are pastors who wish to assume the position of associate or senior associate in order to devote themselves to more pastoral duties and, thus, assume fewer administrative activities. Several dioceses have established the position of vicar for senior priests. From this position, a priest, assigned full or part time, assists priests who are about to retire or those already in retirement.

These very sketchy descriptions of pastoral support systems are intended to underscore the point made at the beginning of this section: pastors need and deserve adequate support and affirmation.

---

19. The National Conference of Catholic Bishops has determined that the term of office for a pastor, for dioceses who wish to establish a set term, is six years and is renewable for six additional years.

20. See *Fullness in Christ.*

# V. The Future: The Challenge to Continue

The process of transformation and change that has affected the role of pastor for the past twenty years will continue. As pastoral realities, needs, and trends change, so too will the role of pastor.

Two reasons have prompted the Committee on Priestly Life and Ministry to look at the future of the pastorate. The first is the fact that current, already discernible trends will continue to have significant impact on the role of the pastor. An orderly identification of these trends and projections may help pastors to sort out the demands of the future and adjust to the still changing reality of American parish life.

The second, and more significant, reason is that the future of the pastorate will not be shaped exclusively by current and discernible trends. It will be shaped by the decisions of bishops, pastors, and dioceses in response to those trends. To a limited extent, the future can be created by a series of choices based on values and beliefs that are shared and actively promoted.

The realities described here that are shaping the future are deliberately called "trends" and not "predictions." They are realities that have already established new patterns of parish life. Their influence will continue to grow. They will continue, also, to influence the work of pastors. There are pioneering pastors and dioceses, scattered throughout the United States, who have already grasped the significance of these trends and have responded to them.

These reflections on the future will concentrate on three distinct or interrelated trends: ( 1 ) the changing profile of the American parish; (2) the changing resources for parish staffing; (3) the changes in parish status and leadership structures.

These three trends are interrelated to the extent that they exert significant impact on each other. Like any organic system, a change in one component inevitably impacts upon all others. To the degree that they can be separated, these trends will be analyzed in light of the effect they will have on the role of the pastor in the parish.

These reflections will be presented in a dual format: a presentation of trends, followed by a description of specific challenges that the trend presents to pastors, bishops, and dioceses. The trend statement will be brief, and documentation of the trend, where available, will be cited in footnotes. The challenge to the pastor will be stated in the form of needed changes and adjustments.

## A. The Trend: The Changing Profile of the American Parish

The trends already noted in the first part of this document are expected to persist. The migration of Catholic peoples in the United States from the Northeast and Midwest to the South and Southwest will continue.[21] The changing ethnic character of the Catholic Church will reflect an increasingly large number of Hispanics, while smaller ethnic populations such as Asians, Haitians, and Poles will continue to grow. The Catholic population, like the American population in general, will be older and require an increased level of attention and pastoral service. The younger generation of Catholics are often perceived by pastors as developing unique characteristics. The better-educated Catholic appears to be developing what might be called a spirit of "selective compliance." This spirit is discernible in the change in the patterns of Mass attendance and in the way

---

21. See *Catholic Church Personnel in the United States,* A report on the Task Force on Church Personnel. It summarizes the data from the National Catholic Directory on Catholic population from 1960-1980 and shows a decrease in New England and the Midwest (Washington, D.C.: National Conference of Catholic Bishops, 1984), p. 9.

in which many respond to the Church's teaching on sexual ethics, birth control, and divorce.[22]

## The Challenge: Evangelization as well as Pastoral Service

Pastors can seldom control the forces that are changing the American parish. They can, however, respond creatively.

Those in the Northeast and Midwest will need to adapt to a smaller number of people in the parish community. Smaller communities will demand more cooperation and collaboration with neighboring parishes as it becomes less feasible to support a full parish-service structure. As population centers shift, and some communities grow smaller, people will experience psychologically and spiritually painful adjustments.

An illustration of this kind of adjustment is the experience of many small rural, farming communities, especially in the Midwest and the Great Plains. As the family farm is dying as a way of life, the adjustments of the community are excruciating. Pastors in these areas understand the need to respond sensitively and spiritually to this "death experience." From all indicators, these trends will continue. In addition to making adjustments to unchangeable realities, parishes may well become the center of community efforts to respond and to change social conditions.

Pastors in areas of the country that are experiencing rapid growth will be faced with a different set of problems. They will be struggling to establish fundamental pastoral services and basic programs, even as they try to articulate parish mission and direction in an atmosphere of great urgency. Growth and expansion present unique opportunities to develop the tested structures of mutual collaboration and participative parish life.

---

22. For a brief discussion on the educated young Catholic, see *Notre Dame Study of Catholic Parish Life*, Report 3 (University of Notre Dame: Institute for Pastoral and Social Ministry, April 1985). For further discussion of the acceptance by American Catholics of the institutional Church's moral teaching on sexuality see Andrew Greely, *American Catholics since the Council: An Unauthorized Report* (Chicago: The Thomas More Press, 1985), pp. 80-100.

In both decline and growth areas the methodologies of pastoral planning may prove to be valuable tools in promoting orderly decline or growth. These methodologies are especially effective in the call for collaboration by clergy and lay leadership alike.

In relation to the changing ethnic character of the American parish, pastors will build upon their success and the need to introduce new responses. Since many groups of newly arrived Catholics are not bringing native clergy with them, many pastors will be required to become bilingual as they are exposed to diverse cultures. Active vocation programs among the new ethnic groups will surface indigenous leadership if pursued vigorously. The struggle with the question of homogenization into the American culture or maintenance of distinctive cultural values will continue to be debated and resolved in various ways. Liturgical and prayer style adaptations to different cultures will surely continue and be even more fruitful.

Pastors will experience more urgency to serve the needs of the growing senior-citizen community. Pastoral care in the home will expand, and, where feasible and economically practical, parish communities may sponsor residence alternatives for their senior members. Parishes that are primarily dependent on the senior-citizen population for financial support will experience fiscal problems as that generation is not replaced by active church supporters.

In addition to expanding services of pastoral care and residence for senior citizens, pastors will be called upon to formulate an appropriate spirituality for what is being called "The Third Age." Based on the Church's strong dedication to the dignity of the individual and the sacredness of life, a more profound appreciation for the gift of extended life will emerge. Seeing its seniors as "gift" and inviting them to share their wisdom and experience with the whole community will serve as a strong counterpoint to a secular culture still obsessed with youth and staying young.[23]

The problems that underlie the changes in patterns of Mass attendance are very complex. Pastors realize that there is a fundamental change in the definition of affiliation with parishes. The current efforts to welcome people back to the Church will need to be expanded dramatically; with active involvement of parish-

---

23. This Christian philosophy of "The Third Age" and its practical and pastoral implications are being developed by the Center for the Third Age, Fordham University, New York.

ioners in encouraging Catholic neighbors to worship, parish attendance will increase. The urgency to focus the attention of young
people on the central importance of participation in the Sunday
Eucharist will become increasingly significant for pastors and their
staffs. Also, the already successful structured efforts at youth involvement in the spiritual and worship life of the parish will need
to be expanded.

The phenomena mentioned here indicate the need for a reex-
amination of the fundamental assumption that is at the root of
American Catholic parish life. The parish in American experience
was established and existed mainly to serve the needs of the Catholic faithful. The Catholic Church followed the migration patterns
of Catholic people, especially the large number of Catholic immigrants in the nineteenth and early twentieth centurys. Under
those conditions, the fundamental purpose of the parish was to
render pastoral service. The Catholic Church and Catholic parishes
were seldom evangelical or oriented toward inclusion and encouragement of new memberships.

While the "service model" of parish will remain the dominant
one in growth areas, the need for an evangelizing or evangelical
model will become even more intense in other parts of the country.
In those areas where Catholic population is in decline, or where
Catholic people are responding on a partial basis to the demands
of the faith, pastors will inevitably be led to the development of
more effective methods of outreach and evangelization. Histori-
cally, Catholic pastors have not been strong evangelical ministers.
In fact, many have shown a distinct distaste for this method of
preaching and parish organization. However, the fundamental
changes in Catholic parish communities may well lead pastors to
create distinctively Catholic forms of evangelization and outreach.

The question of evangelization in the Hispanic community is
even more poignant and pressing. A constant theme of any discussion of Catholic life within the Hispanic church in this country
focuses on the growing problem of fundamentalism and its attrac-
tion to the Hispanic population.

## B. The Trend: Changing Resources for Parish Staffing

There are indications that the decline in the number of ordained priests available for parish service may continue, at least in

some areas.[24] Where possible, dioceses will have to reassign priests from administrative and educational ministries into parish ministry and pastor positions. There are already indications that some local bishops will no longer require retirement for pastors at the age of sixty-five or seventy, as currently stated in retirement policies for many dioceses. Rather, they will allow pastors to continue to the age of seventy-five and, in some cases, even longer.

All indicators are that the permanent diaconate will continue to grow but at a more moderate pace.[25] The continued establishment of lay ministry training programs for full-time professional ministers and volunteers indicates that the numbers of lay professionals and volunteers will continue to increase and the quality of their formation will improve.[26]

## The Challenge: Continued Adjustment to New Resources

The continued decline in the number of ordinations will lead pastors to reassess vocational recruitment as a parish priority and encourage active parish participation in the discernment and the encouragement of vocations. In addition to encouraging vocations, pastors will, in all likelihood, educate the members of their communities about the implications of the priest shortage.

The transition of priests from administrative and educational posts to pastoral positions will be a phenomenon that will continue for several years. In fairness to these men, dioceses will need to offer training and orientation programs in parish and pastoral ministry. If the pastorate is indeed a specialized ministry, special preparation is particularly imperative for those who have had no full-time experience of it.

---

24. See Richard A. Schoenherr and Anamette Sorensen, *Decline and Change in the U.S. Catholic Church* (Madison: University of Wisconsin, 1981).

25. *Annual Report on the Permanent Diaconate* (Washington, D.C.: NCCB Committee on the Permanent Diaconate, 1985).

26. See NCCB Committee on the Laity and NCCB/USCC Office of Research, *Preparing Laity for Ministry: A Directory of Programs in the Catholic Dioceses throughout the United States,* Suzanne E. Elsesser, researcher/editor (Washington, D.C.: USCC Office of Publishing and Promotion Services, 1986).

When diocesan retirement and pension programs were initiated, the usual retirement age for priests was seventy years. In many cases, retirement at age sixty-five was an option. With the revised Code of Canon Law suggesting seventy-five as the age for a pastor to submit his resignation from his position, local bishops, while continuing to allow retirement in accord with their diocesan plans, will allow and even encourage priests to think of this older age as a normal time for their retirement from full pastoral life. While some pastors will welcome this extension of service, many others will resent being used as a stop-gap measure to solve the clergy shortage problem. Bishops and presbyteral councils will need to assess the impact of retirement policies on the morale and performance of pastors.[27]

With fewer priests available for assignment, the policy of "term of office" for pastors may well need to be reviewed. It will continue to be a legitimate method for introducing new pastoral leadership into parish communities and offering a priest a variety of assignment experiences. However, the practical difficulties, especially in smaller dioceses, may lead to reassessment of automatic implementation of term-of-office policies.

The decline in the number of priests available for assignment will have both personal and professional effects on pastors. Fewer priests available for parish assignment inevitably means that the function of the priest and pastor must change. There will be fewer parochial vicars. The logical tendency will be to focus the pastor's ministry in the area of the administration of sacraments, where he is the indispensable and only minister. For the past thirty years, there has been an effort to give a wide definition to the role of the priest as pastor. Should that role be confined to the administration of the sacraments and preaching, most pastors will experience significant adjustment problems. The limitation of their ministries may not be an attractive option, especially for those who have been accustomed to defining their role in very broad terms.

Given the increase in the numbers of permanent deacons and lay ministers, it will be a genuine challenge to the ingenuity of pastors to forge new relationships and to give significant leadership

---

27. In November 1987, as mandated by c. 538 of the revised *Code of Canon Law*, the National Conference of Catholic Bishops will consider *Norms Regarding Retirement for Presbyters*, developed by its Committee on Priestly Life and Ministry and its Committee on Canonical Affairs.

roles to deacons and lay ministers. Continued ambivalence about the roles and functions of these ministers has led to some lack of focus in regard to the training, preparation, and certification of lay ministers. Clarity of role, however, will assist clarity of preparation and formation. As mentioned previously, this will involve time and patience on the part of all.

Pastors will need to take the lead in developing more appropriate compensation systems, geared to the needs of lay ministers and religious. Salaries and benefits received for parish service will have to reflect the different level of need of married lay ministers, deacons, and religious who have dependent senior sisters, brothers, or priests to support. Other issues pastors will need to give sensitive attention to are job security and professional advancement, especially for lay ministers. Related to these personnel questions is the issue of assignment. Many professional lay and religious ministers are hired on a contract basis, while permanent deacons are assigned. Questions of assignment versus hiring and certification versus ordination will, in all likelihood, be determined at the diocesan level, but the impact will be experienced at the parish level.

As lay men and women and married couples become more a part of parish staff, pastors will be asked to help develop a unique lay ministry spirituality. In serving as pastor to his staff as well as to his people, a pastor will need to respond to the circumstances of lay and family life. He is in a unique position to help ministers to resolve some of the tensions between their ministry and personal and family lives and to assist them in capturing the spiritual dimension of their ministerial functions.

## C. The Trend: Changes in Parish Status and Leadership Structures

Current and anticipated changes in parish structures and status are related closely to the two trends described above. It is inevitable that some parishes will close; some will become missions; some will be consolidated with neighboring parishes.

Currently, the preferred method of restructuring seems to be clustering of parishes, maintaining some distinct identity for the parish community but reducing or sharing pastoral services with neighboring parishes.[28] The sharing extends to staff and pastoral leadership. In many clustered communities, deacons as well as lay and religious nonordained administrators will be appointed or assigned to leadership positions.

## The Challenge: Leading the Community to New Life

The most demanding task for pastors will be in cases of the closing and consolidation of parishes or the reduction of a parish to mission status. Pastors will inevitably feel that they are abandoning the community they serve, no matter how small or how much in need of reorganization that community is. Peoples' anger and frustration at being neglected will be felt sharply by pastors who must close or consolidate parishes.

The brief experience to date suggests strongly that closings and consolidations should be executed only with effective diocesan support and implemented through an orderly process of education and consultation. Parish communities simply do not want to die. It is possible, however, to assist members of a community to come to a realistic assessment of their limitations and their need to regroup in relationship to other parish communities. Using an orderly process is tedious and takes time, but it is far preferable to arbitrary decision making.

The process of clustering will require not only adjustment but creative adaptation on the part of pastors. Clustering usually implies that the priest/pastor will minister to several parishes. This possibility is clearly envisioned in the revised *Code of Canon Law,* c. 517. This canon foresees the structuring of the pastoral care of a parish or several parishes by a team of priests or the structure of several parishes under the pastoral supervision of a priest/pastor being entrusted to a deacon or another minister for immediate pastoral service. In addition to the personal adjustment mentioned above, creation of effective relationships, opportunities for com-

---

28. Ms. Suzanne E. Elsesser drew this conclusion in her presentation at the May 1986 "Symposium on Alternate Ways of Staffing Today's Parish," held in Glenview, Illinois.

munication, and direct service to the various parish communities will be needed.

The danger inherent and already observable in the parish clustering is the potential marginalization of the priest/pastor.[29] As deacons and lay ministers become the immediate providers of pastoral services, the priest/pastor can become peripheral to the day-to-day life of the clustered parish community.

---

29. This danger was pointed out by Rev. Bertram Griffin in his remarks at the "Symposium on Alternate Ways of Staffing Today's Parish."

# VI. A New Prologue

The list of trends affecting and shaping the future of the pastorate could be lengthened. However, the purpose in describing these few has been to underscore the obvious fact that the pastorate will continue to experience change and reformulation.

Both the reflections on the past twenty years and the projections into the future make it very clear that pastors throughout the parishes in the United States have played and must continue to play an active and creative role in shaping their own ministry. They have found the source of their inspiration in the Scriptures, in the teaching of the Second Vatican Council, and in the goodness and needs of their people. They have inspired and challenged each other.

Because pastors themselves are so actively and vitally involved in the process of the development of their role, this Committee would like to bring these reflections to a close not by drawing a final conclusion but by issuing an invitation.

We invite the pastors in the 18,900 parishes throughout the United States —individually, but more ideally in small groups—to prolong and deepen the reflections found here. We issue this invitation, not because there are no significant and timely conclusions to be drawn. Indeed, there are already many conclusive observations scattered throughout this text. We extend the invitation to continue these reflections because of our conviction that some of the most important issues have not yet been explored; some of the most significant questions have not been raised.

What has been written here centers mainly on the functional, practical, and ministerial dimensions of the pastor's life and, to a

51

lesser extent, on the personal and spiritual implications of his ministry. All of these issues are not only relevant to pastors themselves but are of central concern to the Catholic people of the parishes of this country. Studying what a pastor does helps to clarify and strengthen his role; it also leads inevitably to more profound questions: What does a pastor stand for? What is his religious significance in the community of faith? What has been described here is, in a sense, an experience in search of theological expression and spiritual meaning.

In the course of our own deliberations, we have rediscovered the fundamental truth that the spiritual leadership of the pastor in the Church today is what spiritual leadership of the people of God has always been—a sign of contradiction.

In our biblical and ecclesial tradition, religious leaders, whether they be judges, prophets, kings, elders, or apostles have always been perceived as religious symbols. The pastorate takes on a symbolic meaning, as well as having a practical utilitarian purpose. The pastor in the parish today becomes—whether he knows and likes it or not—a religious symbol to his people.

The pastor becomes a religious symbol of tradition, the keeper and speaker of the revealed Word in all of its rich expressions. He becomes the religious symbol of God's care for his people, expressing compassions for the wounded and outrage at injustice. He becomes the religious symbol of order, calling the community to an effective stewardship of its gifts and shared use of its resources.

The religious and symbolic significance of the role of the pastor is also a touchstone for understanding the spiritual implications for pastors themselves. As a key religious figure in a community of faith, the pastor experiences both the darkness and the light that are part of every Christian experience. Karl Rahner has attempted to characterize the unique spirituality of pastors under two headings: "the loneliness of faith" and it's dialectical counterpart "the fraternal fellowship of faith."[30] In many ways, our present culture no longer automatically esteems and affirms the person of the pastor. Rather, in pointed ways, it often communicates the message that his ministry has become irrelevant. The decision of pastors to lead and live by faith requires a more radical choice, one less and less affirmed by current culture and more and more grounded in

---

30. Karl Rahner, *Theological Investigations,* vol. XIX (New York: Crossroads, 1983), pp. 47-102.

the "experience of God, of His Spirit, His freedom bursting out of the intermost center of human existence...."[31] The loneliness of this personal, painful and, yet, fundamental religious experience has as its counterpoint the equally compelling experience of spiritual fellowship with other believers. As he leads common worship, as he celebrates important sacramental moments with families, and as he consoles the sick and dying, the pastor experiences the bond of the Spirit with others, and his own faith finds an echo and an enriching response.

We believe that, if pastors themselves begin to explore these dimensions of the religious and spiritual significance of their role, they will begin, at the same time, to write a new and profound prologue to the ministry of the future.

We stand deeply in debt to the pastors of our parish communities for what they have accomplished in the past twenty years. We confidently anticipate their own response to our reflections on their accomplishments by their creative continuation of what is begun here.

31. Ibid., p. 99.

# Appendix A: Pastors and Parishes in the Revised *Code of Canon Law*

The revised *Code of Canon Law*, in chapter VI, deals with pastors and parishes. There are significant differences from the *Code* of 1917.

The following is reprinted, with permission, from *The Code of Canon Law: A Text and Commentary*, commissioned by the Canon Law Society of America and edited by James A. Coriden, Thomas J. Green, and Donald E. Heintschel.

## Parishes

Canon 515,1. A parish is a definite community of the Christian faithful established on a stable basis within a particular church; the pastoral care of the parish is entrusted to a pastor as its own shepherd under the authority of the diocesan bishop.

2. The diocesan bishop alone is competent to erect, suppress or notably alter parishes; he is not to erect, supress or notably alter them without hearing the presbyteral council.

3. A legitimately erected parish has juridic personality by the law itself.

## Quasi-Parish/Other Communities

Canon 516,1. Unless the law provides otherwise, a quasi-parish is equivalent to a parish; a quasi-parish is a definite community of the Christian faithful within a particular church which has been entrusted to a priest as its proper pastor but due to particular circumstances has not yet been erected as a parish.

2. When certain communities cannot be erected as a parish or quasi-parish, the diocesan bishop is to provide for their pastoral care in another manner.

### Team Ministry

Canon 517,1. When circumstances require it, the pastoral care of a parish or of several parishes together can be entrusted to a team of several priests *in solidum* with the requirement, however, that one of them should be the moderator in exercising pastoral care, that is, he should direct their combined activity and answer for it to the bishop.

2. If the diocesan bishop should decide that due to a dearth of priests a participation in the exercise of the pastoral care of a parish is to be entrusted to a deacon or to some other person who is not a priest or to a community of persons, he is to appoint some priest endowed with the powers and faculties of a pastor to supervise the pastoral care.

### Types of Parishes

Canon 518. As a general rule a parish is to be territorial, that is, it embraces all the Christian faithful within a certain territory; whenever it is judged useful, however, personal parishes are to be established based upon rite, language, the nationality of the Christian faithful within some territory or even upon some other determining factor.

### Pastor

Canon 519. The pastor is the proper shepherd of the parish entrusted to him, exercising pastoral care in the community entrusted to him under the authority of the diocesan bishop in whose ministry of Christ he has been called to share; in accord with the norm of law he carries out for his community the duties of teaching, sanctifying and governing, with the cooperation of other presbyters or deacons and the assistance of lay members of the Christian faithful.

## Parishes Entrusted to Religious

Canon 520,1. A juridic person is not to be a pastor: however, the diocesan bishop, but not the diocesan administrator, with the consent of the competent superior, can entrust a parish to a clerical religious institute or to a clerical society of apostolic life, even erecting the parish in a church of the institute or society, with the requirement, however, that one presbyter should be the pastor of the parish or one presbyter should act as the moderator mentioned in c. 517,1 if its pastoral care is entrusted to a team.

2. The assignment of the parish mentioned in c. 520,1. can be permanent or for a definite predetermined period of time; in either case the assignment should be made by means of a written agreement between the diocesan bishop and the competent superior of the institute or society; among other matters this agreement is expressly and carefully to determine the work to be done, the persons to be attached to the parish and the financial arrangements.

## Qualifications for Pastors

Canon 521,1. To assume the office of pastor validly one must be in the sacred order of the presbyterate.

2. He should also be distinguished for his sound doctrine and integrity of morals and endowed with a zeal for souls and other virtues; he should also possess those qualities which are required by universal and particular law to care for the parish in question.

3. For the office of pastor to be conferred on someone, it is necessary that his suitability be clearly evident by means of some method determined by the diocesan bishop, even by means of an examination.

## Term of Office for Pastors

Canon 522. The pastor ought to possess stability in office and therefore he is to be named for an indefinite period of time; the diocesan bishop can name him for a certain period of time only if a decree of the conference of bishops has permitted this.

## Assignment of Pastor

Canon 523. With due regard for the prescription of c. 682,1, the diocesan bishop is the person competent to provide for the office

57

of pastor by means of free conferral unless someone possesses the right of presentation or of election.

## Suitability of Pastor

Canon 524. After he has weighed all the circumstances, the diocesan bishop is to confer a vacant parish on the person whom he judges suited to fulfill its parochial care without any partiality; in order to make a judgment concerning a person's suitability he is to listen to the vicar forane, conduct appropriate investigations and, if it is warranted, listen to certain presbyters and lay members of the Christian faithful.

## Pastoral Appointments during Impeded/Vacant Diocese

Canon 525. When a see is vacant or impeded, the diocesan administrator or another person who is ruling the diocese in the meantime is competent:

    1. to install or confirm presbyters who have been legitimately presented or elected for a parish;

    2. to appoint pastors if the see has been vacant or impeded for a year.

## One Pastor Only

Canon 526,1. A pastor is to have the parochial care of only one parish; however the care of several neighboring parishes can be entrusted to the same pastor due to a dearth of priests or in other circumstances.

    2. In the same parish there is to be only one pastor or one moderator in accord with c. 517,1; any custom contrary to this is reprobated and any privilege contrary to this is revoked.

## Installation of Pastor

Canon 527,1. The person who has been promoted to carry out the pastoral care of a parish acquires that care and is bound to exercise it from the moment he takes possession of the parish.

    2. While observing the method accepted by particular law or legitimate custom, the local ordinary or a priest delegated by him places the pastor in possession of the parish; for a just cause, however, the same ordinary can dispense from such a method of in-

58

stallation; in such a situation the notification of the dispensation communicated to the parish replaces the formal taking of possession.

3. The local ordinary is to define a period of time within which the parish is to be taken possession of; if the time lapses needlessly and there be no legitimate impediment, he can declare the parish vacant.

## The Pastor as Teacher and Sanctifier

Canon 528,1. The pastor is obliged to see to it that the word of God in its entirety is announced to those living in the parish; for this reason he is to see to it that the lay Christian faithful are instructed in the truths of the faith, especially through the homily which is to be given on Sundays and holy days of obligation and through the catechetical formation which he is to give; he is to foster works by which the spirit of the gospel, including issues involving social justice, is promoted; he is to take special care for the Catholic education of children and of young adults; he is to make every effort with the aid of the Christian faithful, to bring the gospel message also to those who have ceased practicing their religion or who do not profess the true faith.

2. The pastor is to see to it that the Most Holy Eucharist is the center of the parish assembly of the faithful; he is to work to see to it that the Christian faithful are nourished through a devout celebration of the sacraments and especially that they frequently approach the sacrament of the Most Holy Eucharist and the sacrament of penance; he is likewise to endeavor that they are brought to the practice of family prayer as well as to a knowing and active participation in the sacred liturgy, which the pastor must supervise in his parish under the authority of the diocesan bishop, being vigilant lest any abuses creep in.

## Pastor's Obligations: Governance

Canon 529,1. In order to fulfill his office in earnest, the pastor should strive to come to know the faithful who have been entrusted to his care; therefore he is to visit families, sharing the cares, worries, and especially the griefs of the faithful, strengthening them in the Lord, and correcting them prudently if they are wanting in certain areas; with a generous love he is to help the sick, particularly those close to death, refreshing them solicitously with the sacraments

59

and commending their souls to God; he is to make a special effort to seek out the poor, the afflicted, the lonely, those exiled from their own land, and similarly those weighed down with special difficulties; he is also to labor diligently so that spouses and parents are supported in fulfilling their proper duties, and he is to foster growth in the Christian life within the family.

2. The pastor is to acknowledge and promote a proper role which the lay members of the Christian faithful have in the Church's mission by fostering their associations for religious purposes; he is to cooperate with his own bishop and with the presbyterate of the diocese in working hard so that the faithful be concerned for parochial communion and that they realize that they are members both of the diocese and of the universal Church and participate in and support efforts to promote such communion.

### Functions of the Parish Priest

Canon 530. The following functions are especially entrusted to the pastor:
1. the administration of baptism;
2. the administration of the sacrament of confirmation to those who are in danger of death, according to the norm of c. 883,3;
3. the administration of Viaticum and the anointing of the sick with due regard for the prescription of c. 1003,2 and 3, as well as the imparting of the apostolic blessing;
4. the assistance at marriages and the imparting of the nuptial blessing;
5. the performing of funerals;
6. the blessing of the baptismal font during the Easter season, the leading of processions outside the church and the imparting of solemn blessings outside the church;
7. the more solemn celebration of the Eucharist on Sundays and holy days of obligation.

### Stole Fees

Canon 531. Although another person may have performed some parochial function, that person is to put the offerings received from the Christian faithful on that occasion into the parish account, unless it is obvious that such would be contrary to the will of the donor in the case of voluntary offerings; after he has listened to the presbyteral council, the diocesan bishop is competent to issue regulations which provide for the allocation of these offerings and the remuneration of clerics who fulfill the same function.

## Juridic Representation of the Parish

Canon 532. The pastor represents the parish in all juridic affairs in accord with the norm of law; he is to see to it that the goods of the parish are administered in accord with the norms of cc. 1281-1288.

## Residency, Vacation and Absence of Pastors

Canon 533,1. The pastor is obliged to reside in a parish house close to the church; in particular cases, however, the local ordinary can permit him to live elsewhere, especially in a house shared by several presbyters, provided there is a just cause and suitable and due provision is made for the performance of parochial functions.

2. Unless there is a serious reason to the contrary, the pastor may be absent each year from the parish on vacation for at most one continuous or interrupted month; the days which the pastor spends once a year in spiritual retreat are not counted in his vacation days; if the pastor is to be absent from the parish beyond a week he is bound to inform the local ordinary of this.

3. The diocesan bishop is to issue norms which provide for the care of a parish by a priest possessing the needed faculties during the absence of the pastor.

## Mass for the People

Canon 534,1. After he has taken possession of his parish the pastor is obliged to apply Mass for the people entrusted to him each Sunday and holy day of obligation within the diocese; if he is legitimately prevented from this celebration, he is to apply Mass on these same days through another priest or he himself is to apply it on other days.

2. A pastor who has the care of several parishes is obliged to apply only one Mass for all the people entrusted to him on those days mentioned in c. 534,1.

3. A pastor who has not satisfied the obligation mentioned in c. 534,1 and 2 is to apply as many Masses for his people as he has missed as soon as possible.

## Parish Registers

Canon 535,1. Each parish is to possess a set of parish books including baptismal, marriage and death registers as well as other registers prescribed by the conference of bishops or the diocesan bishop; the pastor is to see to it that these registers are accurately inscribed and carefully preserved.

2. In the baptismal register are also to be noted the person's confirmation and whatever affects the canonical status of the Christian faithful by reason of marriage, with due regard for the prescription of c. 1133, adoption, reception of sacred orders, perpetual profession in a religious institute, and change of rite; these notations are always to be noted on a document which certifies the reception of baptism.

3. Each parish is to possess its own seal; documents which are issued to certify the canonical status of the Christian faithful as well as all acts which can have juridic importance are to be signed by the pastor or his delegate and sealed with the parish seal.

4. Each parish is to have a registry or archive in which the parish books are kept along with episcopal letters and other documents which ought to be preserved due to necessity or usefulness; all these are to be inspected by the diocesan bishop or his delegate during his visitation or at another suitable time; the pastor is to take care that they do not come into the hands of outsiders.

5. The older parish books are also to be carefully preserved in accord with the prescriptions of particular law.

## Parish Councils

Canon 536,1. After the diocesan bishop has listened to the presbyteral council and if he judges it opportune, a pastoral council is to be established in each parish; the pastor presides over it, and through it the Christian faithful along with those who share in the pastoral care of the parish in virtue of their office give their help in fostering pastoral activity.

2. This pastoral council possesses a consultative vote only and is governed by norms determined by the diocesan bishop.

## Parish Finance Council

Canon 537. Each parish is to have a finance council which is regulated by universal law as well as by norms issued by the diocesan bishop; in this council the Christian faithful, selected according to the same norms, aid the pastor in the administration of parish goods with due regard for the prescription of c. 532.

## Cessation from the Pastoral Office and Retirement

Canon 538,1. A pastor ceases from office by means of removal or transfer by the diocesan bishop which has been done in accord with the norm of law, by resignation of the pastor submitted for a just cause and accepted by the same diocesan bishop for validity and by lapse of time if the pastor has been appointed for a definite period of time in accord with the prescriptions of particular law mentioned in c. 522.

2. A pastor who is a member of a religious institute or a society of apostolic life is removed in accord with the norm of c. 682,2.

3. When a pastor has completed his seventy-fifth year of age he is asked to submit his resignation from office to the diocesan bishop, who, after considering all the circumstances of person and place, is to decide whether to accept or defer the resignation; the diocesan bishop, taking into account the norms determined by the conference of bishops, is to provide for the suitable support and housing of the resigned pastor.

## Impeded or Vacant Parish

Canon 539. When a parish becomes vacant or when the pastor is prevented from exercising his pastoral office in the parish due to captivity, exile, banishment, incapacity, ill health or some other cause, the diocesan bishop is to appoint as soon as possible a parochial administrator, that is, a priest who substitutes for the pastor in accord with the norm of c. 540.

## Parochial Administrator

Canon 540,1. A parochial administrator is bound by the same duties and enjoys the same rights as a pastor unless the diocesan bishop determines otherwise.

2. A parochial administrator is not permitted to do anything which can prejudice the rights of the pastor or harm parish goods.

3. After he has fulfilled his function, the parochial administrator is to render an account to the pastor.

### Parish Vacancy/Pastor Impeded: Interim Governance

Canon 541,1. When a parish becomes vacant or when the pastor is hindered from exercising his pastoral duty the parochial vicar is to assume the governance of the parish in the meantime until a parochial administrator is appointed; if there are several parochial vicars, the senior vicar in terms of appointment assumes the governance; if there are no parochial vicars, then a pastor specified by particular law assumes the governance.

2. The person who has assumed the governance of a parish in accord with the norm of c. 541,1 is to inform the local ordinary immediately that the parish is vacant.

### Qualifications of Team Members

Canon 542. The priests who as a team have been entrusted with the pastoral care of some parish or group of different parishes in accord with the norm of c. 517,1:

1. are to be endowed with the qualities mentioned in c. 521;

2. are to be appointed or installed in accord with the prescriptions of cc. 522 and 524;

3. are responsible for pastoral care only from the moment of taking possession; their moderator is to be placed in possession of the parish in accord with the prescriptions of c. 527,2; for the other priests a legitimately made profession of faith substitutes for taking possession.

### Functions and Duties of Team Members

Canon 543,1. Each of the priests who as a team have been entrusted with the pastoral care of some parish or group of different parishes is obliged to perform the duties and functions of the pastor which are mentioned in cc. 528, 529 and 530 in accord with an arrangement determined by themselves; all these priests possess the faculty to assist at marriages as well as all the faculties to dispense which are granted to the pastor by the law itself, to be exercised, however, under the direction of the moderator.

2. All priests of the team:

1. are bound by the obligation of residence;

2. through common counsel are to establish an arrangement by which one of them celebrates Mass for the people in accord with the norm of c. 534;

3. in the juridic affairs only the moderator represents the parish or parishes entrusted to the team.

## Vacancy on the Team

Canon 544. When one of the priests in the team mentioned in c. 517,1 or its moderator ceases from office or when one of them becomes incapable of exercising pastoral duties the parish or parishes entrusted to the care of the team do not become vacant; however, the diocesan bishop is to name another moderator; the senior priest on the team in terms of assignment is to fulfill the office of moderator until another is appointed by the diocesan bishop.

# Appendix B: A Statement on Growth in Ministry through Ministerial Accountability and Performance Evaluation

The following is an excerpt from *Ministerial Performance Evaluation of Catholic Clergy in the Diocese of Cleveland,* a thesis for the degree of Doctor of Ministry, by Rev. Robert F. Pfeiffer, United Theological Seminary, Dayton, Ohio.

1. Priests are responsible for the transmission of the reality of Jesus Christ as Lord. Jesus has called them to minister in the Church in a special way, in order to facilitate the Spirit's work in bringing people to holiness. "They share in his ministry, whereby the Church here on earth is unceasingly built into the People of God, the Body of Christ, and the Temple of the Holy Spirit." Thus, it is to Christ that priests are primarily responsible, for he has called them to share his ministry of proclamation and reconciliation. Likewise, they serve a Church which is his, a people who are his own.

2. As a priest fulfills this ministry and undertakes various assignments, he will naturally ask what is expected of him, by what criteria he might be measured and evaluated, how judgment might be made concerning the accomplishment of his sacred trust, and how and to whom he is accountable.

## Accountability for All Priests

3. The Scriptures describe people as accountable before God. The central theme of "covenant" in both Old and New Testaments

is essentially a theme of accountability (Mt 5:13-16; 25:34-40) and insists that they manage their talents well (Mt 25:14-30). Saint Paul develops this theme from two different perspectives in Romans 2 and 3, and also in 2 Corinthians 5:10. Against this Scripture background, accountability can be seen as an ongoing dialogue in relation to man's partnership with God.

4. Within the structure of the Church, the priest is accountable to Christ and to the Church for his ministry, for priestly ministry is not an end in itself. It is a mission received, exercised always "in" Christ, "to" the people, and "for" the kingdom.

5. The priest is also accountable to himself for his personal growth and self-development, for his use and enrichment of his talents and skills, and for his accomplishment of the ministry that has been entrusted to his care and fulfillment.

6. Accountability in the priesthood finds its basis in these understandings. The priest is a part of the Church's ministry, assisting in the achievement of its mission, and he should contribute to this mission in a functional way (not in a manner which is dysfunctional).

7. A process of accountability is intended, therefore, to assist such functional activity and to promote its development and continuance. It can be seen as that process by which a priest is expected to answer for doing specific things, according to specific plans and criteria, in order to accomplish specific results related to the Church's purpose.

8. A program of ministerial evaluation can be of great assistance to the priest in fulfilling this responsibility to be accountable for the growth and performance of his ministry. It offers him the opportunity to reflect upon his growth in his understanding of the Church's mission and of her expectations of the priesthood. He also has the opportunity to become more understanding of himself, of his individual worth, and of his special contribution to the ministry as a whole. Thus, his response to this ministry and his own personal growth can be greatly enhanced through his being accountable.

### The Bishop and His Priests

9. Because the bishop is placed at the summit of the sacred ministry, he is accountable for the evaluation of the ministry in his diocese, and he is responsible for the management of the Church's

greatest asset, the talent and zeal of those who devote their total service to the preaching of the Gospel.

10. As bishop, he must make important decisions concerning his personnel. Hence, he must employ some means to measure ministerial effectiveness; and the correctness of his judgment will depend, to a large extent, on the accuracy of these evaluations.

11. Thus, a process of ministerial evaluation can be of great assistance to the bishop in making the personnel decisions which are his responsibility.

## Performance Evaluation

12. A process of performance evaluation should be an integral part of the exercise of ministerial accountability. Such a process is intended not only to assist a priest in meeting his responsibilities and to lead him to fuller personal growth and maturity but also to express the Church's concern for this growth and for his individual development as a minister of the Gospel.

13. The program of performance evaluation [contained in Appendix D] is designed to enable a priest to discover both his strengths and weaknesses. Consequently, it can be a great source of positive personal support and encouragement.

14. As the [then] ad hoc Committee for Priestly Life and Ministry of the National Conference of Catholic Bishops has stated:

> We wish an evaluation process which will radiate the personal concern and love of Christ for each individual priest felt and experienced through the action of the Church. We wish an evaluation process which shows a positive concern for each priest as an individual, which assists him to proclaim the Gospel, to set realistic goals for his ministry, to provide him with ongoing opportunities for theological updating, to enable him to perceive himself as always becoming a man who is a meaningful and needed minister of the Gospel in the lives of his people (*The Report of the Bishops' Ad Hoc Committee for Priestly Life and Ministry* Washington, D.C.: Office of Publishing and Promotion Services, 1974, p. 18).

15. With these goals in mind, a ministerial evaluation program is designed to answer questions such as:

a) What does the priest do? What is his ministry?

b) What is he accomplishing? What should he be accomplishing? What could be accomplished?

c) How effective is he? Are his talents, opportunities, and time used well?

d) What knowledge, skills, and talents does this priest have? What does he need to further his ministry?

e) What are the sources of growth and support in this priest's life? Can more be identified and developed?

16. One expected result of such a growth program would also be a growth in morale among the presbyterate. When a priest experiences himself as growing and maturing, when he sees himself becoming more competent and acquiring new skills, when he sets goals and objectives for himself and is able to discern his accomplishments, then he is more comfortable with himself, derives greater satisfaction from his work, and is a more effective priestly minister.

# Appendix C: Goals and Benefits of Ministerial Self-Review

The following is an excerpt from *Ministerial Performance Evaluation of Catholic Clergy in the Diocese of Cleveland,* a thesis for the degree of Doctor of Ministry, by Rev. Robert F. Pfeiffer, United Theological Seminary, Dayton, Ohio.

*Goals:*

1. To help the priest identify his basic ministerial functions in ministry today.
2. To help the priest become more aware of his priorities in ministry.
3. To help the priest become more aware of how he uses his time.
4. To help the priest become more aware of what constitutes effective ministry, that is, the ability to think, plan, and operate in a collaborative manner.
5. To help the priest become more aware of his accountability to himself, to God, and to the Church which he serves.

*Benefits: To the Priest Himself:*

1. Fulfillment of the psychological need for recognition and appreciation.
2. Demonstration of the fact that the Church (bishop, peers, laity) care about him.
3. Allowance for periodic review of personal potential and achievement.

4. Provision of the opportunity for growth and maturity in the Christian community he serves:
   - opportunities to help assess new forms of ministry;
   - opportunities for learning to lessen the gap between the priest and people and the priest and bishop;
   - sharing in the surfacing of special talents of priests;
   - facilitating consensus on setting goals.

# Appendix D: Review of Priestly Ministry

Name: _____

Date: _____

[This instrument seeks to help the parish priest assess the performance of his ministry as a person and as a priest in the context of his ministry.]

---

Instructions: In the space at the left of each item, please indicate by using letters A, B, or C the satisfaction you experience or the degree of help you feel you need in the various areas of ministry.

A  =  I feel very satisfied with my performance.

B  =  I feel somewhat satisfied and would welcome some help.

C  =  I feel dissatisfied and would welcome considerable help.

N/A  =  Not Applicable.

---

A. As a spiritual leader of the parish community and celebrant of Word and sacrament, I feel that I . . .

_____ 1. preside at the eucharistic liturgy with reverence and dignity (including prayerfulness, sensitivity to the people, and encouraging participation).

_____ 2. prepare and plan the liturgies with creative use of appropriate options.

_____a. Sunday liturgies

_____b. Children's liturgies

_____c. Weddings and other sacraments

_____ 3. am comfortable in celebrating the liturgy.

_____ 4. effectively involve other ministers in the liturgy (e.g., lectors, musicians, lay distributors, both men and women).

_____ 5. celebrate the sacrament of baptism, inviting prayerful participation of parents, sponsors, and the parish.

_____ 6. am comfortable in celebrating the new rite of penance (e.g., face-to-face option, Christlike compassion, unhurried).

_____ 7. celebrate the sacrament of the anointing of the sick with sensitivity to individuals and families.

My comments on how I feel about my effectiveness and comfort as celebrant of the Eucharist and of the other sacraments:

_____

_____

_____

As a preacher, I feel that I . . .

_____ 1. prepare my homilies.

_____ 2. preach the gospel message itself; not just my own advice.

_____ 3. address a need or problem the listeners are experiencing in their lives (e.g., Does my homily answer the question "So what?").

_____ 4. share my own personal involvement and struggle with the gospel message.

_____ 5. use good illustrations, stories, and examples.

_____ 6. use a structured process of homily evaluation by receiving feedback from people on a formal and regular basis.

_____ 7. enrich the liturgy by providing introductions, brief homilies, or silent reflections during the week.

_____ 8. have preaching as one of my priorities.

A summary of how I feel about the role of preaching and my effectiveness:

_____

_____

_____

In other areas of spiritual leadership, I feel that I . . .

_____ 1. am willing to provide opportunities for a variety of communal prayer other than Mass (e.g., stations, Liturgy of the Hours, bible services).

_____ 2. participate personally in parish spiritual growth programs (e.g., prayer groups, spiritual renewals).

_____ 3. am willing to accept the responsibility for being a spiritual director.

_____ 4. am comfortable in praying spontaneously with others.

My reflections on how I see the quality of my spiritual leadership:

_____

_____

_____

B. Religious Education in the Parish.

This involves:  a. the teaching of doctrine;
b. the experiencing of Christian community;

    c. providing opportunities of Christian service to
       others.

In the area of religious education, I feel that I . . .

_____ 1. am effectively involved with religious education in the
       parish day school.

_____ 2. am involved with religious education in the parish
       school of religion.

_____ 3. cooperate with religious and lay personnel in the re-
       ligious education program.

_____ 4. am directly involved with children and with adults in
       sacramental preparation programs (e.g., baptism, first
       penance, first Eucharist).

_____ 5. participate in adult religious education (e.g., by teach-
       ing, by providing incentive, planning, direction).

_____ 6. am effective in premarital counseling.

_____ 7. participate in religious enrichment programs for entire
       families.

How I see my role in the total religious education of the parish:

_____

_____

_____

C. As a priest serving the spiritual and human needs of the people,
   I feel that I . . .

_____ 1. minister effectively to the sick, dying, and bereaved
       (e.g., hospitals, nursing homes, shut-ins).

_____ 2. care for the poor of the parish (e.g., food distribution,
       Vincent de Paul).

_____ 3. care for the poor outside the parish (e.g., diocese,
       country).

_____ 4. am competent and comfortable as a counselor.

_____ 5. evangelize the unchurched.

_____ 6. reach out to Catholics who do not attend church regularly.

_____ 7. make an effort to provide services to the non-English-speaking people.

_____ 8. minister effectively to youth outside strictly educational programs.

_____ 9. am available to parishioners (e.g., readiness to answer the phone, make appointments, attend parish functions).

_____ 10. foster a sense of community.

_____ 11. visit the parishioners in their homes.

_____ 12. respond to supraparochial responsibilities (e.g., deanery, diocese).

How I feel about my effectiveness in meeting the spiritual and human needs of the people:

_____

_____

_____

D. The parish priest carries out his duties professionally and in a spirit of collaboration with others.

How effective am I in working with the following persons and groups?

_____ 1. Priests

_____ 2. Religious men and women

_____ 3. Parish council and commissions

_____ 4. Parish employees

_____ 5. Adult lay people

_____ 6. Various parish organizations for which I am responsible

_____ 7. Others: _____

How comfortable do I feel in working with the above persons and groups?

_____

_____

_____

E. The priests of the parish help to make the rectory a home, and they witness a fraternal love for one another. How I feel about...

_____ 1. my personal efforts in creating such an atmosphere.

_____ 2. my participation in shared prayer with the priests in the rectory.

_____ 3. my outreach and support of other priests in the rectory.

_____ 4. my availability in responding to the personal needs of other priests in the diocese (e.g., personal requests, the sick, the retired).

How I feel about priest to priest relationships in the rectory and in the diocese:

_____

_____

_____

F. The parish priest is a leader in the local community. I feel that I am involved in ...

_____ 1. ecumenical activities with neighboring churches.

_____ 2. projects and organizations of the neighborhood and wider civic community.

Comments:

_____

_____

_____

G. Continuing education: I feel that I . . .

_____ 1. participate in continuing education opportunities (e.g., clergy institutes, workshops, courses).

_____ 2. regularly do professional reading (e.g., books, journals).

My specific needs for continuing education at this time:

_____

_____

_____


H. Administrative responsibilities: I feel that I . . .
(for pastors and associates)

_____ 1. have an overall administrative ability.

_____ 2. see to the preparation and use of budgets by persons responsible for various programs.

_____ 3. oversee the condition of the parish plant (e.g., working order, cleanliness).

_____ 4. am accountable and report finances to the parish and the diocese.

_____ 5. allow and encourage others (staff and parishioners) to participate in administrative decisions.

How I feel about administration as a pastoral responsibility:

_____

_____

_____


I. Personal and professional qualities: I feel that I . . .

_____ 1. am dependable and prompt for scheduled appointments, meetings, liturgies, etc.

_____ 2. accept advice and guidance.

_____ 3. set realistic goals for myself.

_____ 4. follow through on projects for which I am responsible.

_____ 5. reflect joy and happiness in my life as a priest.

_____ 6. encourage priestly and religious vocations.

_____ 7. witness the gospel message by my life style.

_____ 8. lead others effectively and harmoniously.

_____ 9. share the workload.

_____ 10. have a good attitude toward my superiors and their use of authority.

_____ 11. am concerned with overall parish needs.

_____ 12. am concerned with the total needs of the area served by the parish.

_____ 13. cooperate on team projects.

_____ 14. like to meet people and enjoy interacting with them.

Comments on my personal and professional qualities:

_____

_____

_____

Description of my dominant emotional state, using some of the following or similar words: relaxed; tense; comfortable; concerned; cheerful; depressed; lighthearted; serious; spontaneous; inhibited; etc.:

_____

_____

_____

J.  Use of time: I feel that I . . .

_____ 1. make effective use of time in ministry.

_____ 2. am responsible in my use of time for recreation.

80

K.  If I had to name any negative factors in the performance of my ministry, they would be . . .

(check any that apply)

___ Inadequacy of preparation

___ Frequent illness

___ Insomnia or Hypersomnia

___ Borderline anxiety

___ Alcohol/drug dependencies

___ Loneliness

___ Other _____

___     _____

___ Lack of energy and enthusiasm

___ Lack of spiritual direction

___ Family responsibilities

___ High expectations of superiors

___ High expectations of parish/colleagues

___ Heavy administrative responsibilities

___ Low self-image

___ Lack of institutional support

Other comments about this review or about any of the previous areas of ministry or about any areas not mentioned:

_____

_____

_____

How much time did it take you to complete this instrument? ___

_____

[Please return this completed instrument to the priest confidant you have selected.]

# Appendix E: Convention of Pastors

The "Convention of Pastors" was born out of a renewed faith in the parish as the place where the hopes of Vatican II will flourish. It was born also out of the conviction that there is a distinct role for the pastor, with identifiable and necessary skills that are critical in enabling parishes to fulfill their mission.

The original design for the "Convention of Pastors" was developed by a team that represented three national organizations: the National Pastoral Planning Conference; the Parish and Diocesan Council Network; and the National Organization for Continuing Education of Roman Catholic Clergy. Their design provided the flexible outline, which can be adapted to the specific needs of a province or region by the directors of continuing formation of that province or region.

The purpose of the "Convention of Pastors" is to assist pastors to deepen the effectiveness of their ministry. A broad range of topics are discussed; workshops are provided on themes such as:

1. Styles of Pastor Leadership
2. Presiding at Liturgy
3. Preparing Effective Homilies
4. Sexuality and Intimacy
5. Conversion and Faith Development in Adults
6. Dealing with Stress
7. The Changing Role and Expectations
8. Relations in a Parish Staff
9. Moral Theology for a Pastoral Minister
10. Principles and Approaches for Parish Spiritual Renewal

11. Constructive Conflict Management
12. Communication Skills
13. Parish Council: Its Structure and Dynamics
14. Parish Planning
15. The Art of the Parish Administration
16. A Theology of Parish
17. Other Suggested Topics as needed

The schedule of the Convention is usually designed according to the expressed interests of the participants, who frequently have the opportunity to attend one of several simultaneous workshops.

The "Convention of Pastors" is currently sponsored by the National Organization of Continuing Education for Roman Catholic Clergy. Further information can be obtained from its national office (5401 South Cornell Avenue, Chicago, IL 60615) or from local directors of continuing formation of priests.